ESCAPING
AUSCHWITZ

ESCAPING
AUSCHWITZ

A CULTURE OF FORGETTING

RUTH LINN

Cornell University Press

Ithaca and London

A volume in the series Psychoanalysis and Social Theory, edited by
C. Fred Alford and James M. Glass

First published 2004 by Cornell University Press

Printed in the United States of America

Library of Congress Cataloging-in-Publication Data
Linn, Ruth.
    Escaping Auschwitz : a culture of forgetting / Ruth Linn.
        p. cm. — (Psychoanalysis and social theory)
    Includes bibliographical references and index.
    ISBN 0-8014-4130-7 (cloth : alk. paper)
    1. Holocaust, Jewish (1939–1945).   2. Holocaust, Jewish (1939–1945)—
Historiography.   3. Holocaust, Jewish (1939–1945)—Moral and ethical aspects.
4. Jews—persecutions—Hungary.   5. Jewish councils—Europe, Eastern—
History—20th century.   6. Arendt, Hannah—Views on the Holocaust.
7. Vrba, Rudolph.   8. Wetzler, Fred.   I. Title.   II. Series.
    D804.3.L57 2004
    940.53′18—dc22
                                                                    2004006702

Cloth printing   10 9 8 7 6 5 4 3 2 1

CONTENTS

ACKNOWLEDGMENTS

"Even if we admit that every generation has the right to write its own history," Hannah Arendt tells us, "we admit no more than that it has the right to rearrange the facts in accordance with its own perspective; we do not admit the right to touch the factual matter itself."[1]

In this book I try to locate and rearrange historical facts regarding the escape from Auschwitz—I do so as an Israeli citizen who never knew there had been such an event.[2]

I owe a special debt of gratitude to the protagonist of this book, Professor Rudolf Vrba, who initially saw no point in talking to an Israeli researcher but who in the end was willing to teach me the Holocaust as seen from the ramp at Auschwitz.

I further owe special thanks to Professor Vrba's wife, Robin, who welcomed me into their home and life's story; my friend Mira Samet, who put me in touch with Vrba; Yehoshua Ben Ami, the translator of Vrba's book; my brother-in-law, Dov Schlein, who was the only one who succeeded in putting me in touch with Mr. George Soros, who then kindly let me question him on his Budapest history and his acquaintance with the Vrba-Wetzler report. Professor George Klein, a member of the Nobel prize committee at the Karolinska Institute in Stockholm, generously gave me his time when I interviewed him in Jerusalem.

Professor Aaron Ben-Ze'ev, rector of the University of Haifa, was the first academician to see the significance of this research. His friendship and support enabled me to pursue this project against a number of odds. The understanding of my English editor, Dick Bruggeman, who helped me revise my manuscript, proved invaluable.

At Cornell University Press, I am grateful to Professors Fred Alford and James Glass, editors of Cornell's Psychoanalysis and Social Theory series, who were both challenging and supportive throughout the revision process; Roger Haydon, senior editor at Cornell, who handled the manuscript with intelligent criticism, care, and encouragement; and Priscilla Hurdle, who prepared my book for publication.

This book would not have seen the light of day without the initial support of a UNESCO grant for the study of resistance and peace and the Rubin Foundation and its president, Cora Weiss, and her belief in courageous political acts of early warning. The friendship of Shirley and Mickey Bloomfield during all my years of university studies has been invaluable to me. This book is one more fruit of this friendship. I dedicate the work to Steven and Sybil Stone, in recognition of their sensitivity to the injustice in this world. Sadly, Steven did not live to see the book in print. May it carry his vision to a new generation.

Last, but not least, there are numerous close friends and family members who escorted me along the way. I hope they will forgive me and understand that I mention here only my small family, for whom the protagonist of this book became part not only of their mom's research but also of their Jewish heritage: Yair, Gilat, and Erez, my kids, and Shai, my husband, who all along stood by me and my failing computer with much love, wisdom, and patience.

RUTH LINN

Haifa

ESCAPING
AUSCHWITZ

INTRODUCTION

It is easier to deny entry to a memory than to free one-
self from it after it has been recorded.

PRIMO LEVI, *The Drowned and the Saved*

On April 7, 1944, Rudolf Vrba managed to escape from Auschwitz-
Birkenau with his friend and fellow inmate, Alfred Wetzler. These
Jewish prisoners had been deported from Slovakia in the spring of
1942. After a perilous eleven days of walking and hiding, the escapees
made it back to their native country, Slovakia. Almost at once, they
managed to establish contact with the leaders of the remainder of the
Jewish community there (about 25,000 of what had been 88,000 souls).
They warned that preparations were being made for the murder of
nearly 800,000 Jews from Hungary. They also suspected that 3,000
Czech Jews, in the Auschwitz-Birkenau "family camp" would be gassed
within a few months.

For three days Vrba and Wetzler conveyed in detail to the members
of the Jewish Council the geographical plan of Auschwitz-Birkenau,
the specifics of the Germans' method of mass murder—tattooing,
gassing, and cremation—and the course of events they had witnessed
at the camp. They gave an estimate of the number of Jews killed in
Auschwitz between June 1942 and April 1944: about 1.75 million.

The Vrba-Wetzler report was uncannily thorough in its accuracy and
detail.[1] It was carefully examined by the official Jewish leadership of
Slovakia.[2] The escapees were assured that the information it contained
would be disseminated without delay to the Western world and, of
course, to the potential victims, who at that time were still freely walk-

ing the streets of Hungary. Vrba's and Wetzler's predictions were soon confirmed by two other Auschwitz inmates, Czeslaw Mordowicz and Arnost Rosin, who succeeded in escaping from Auschwitz on May 27, 1944, and reached Slovakia on June 6, 1944. They reported that during the month of May 1944 Hungarian Jews were being murdered in Auschwitz at an unprecedented rate and that the expanded facilities were fully in use. Human fat was used to accelerate the burning of the corpses.

The Vrba-Wetzler report was the first document about the Auschwitz death camp to reach the free world and to be accepted as credible.[3] Its authenticity broke the barrier of skepticism and apathy that had existed up to that point.[4] It is doubtful, however, that its content reached more than a small number of the prospective victims, though Vrba's and Wetzler's critical and alarming assessment was in the hands of Hungarian Jewish leaders as early as April 28 or at least no later than early May 1944.[5] Between mid-May and early July 1944, about 437,000 Hungarian Jews boarded in good faith the "resettlement trains" that carried them to the Auschwitz death camps, where most were immediately gassed.[6] Yet, memoirs by a handful of surviving Hungarian deportees, even of those who arrived in Auschwitz as late as July 8, 1944, reveal their absolute ignorance of their impending fate at the death camp.[7] Elie Wiesel summarized it as follows: "We were taken just two weeks before D-Day, and we did not know that Auschwitz existed. . . . everyone knew except the victims."[8]

Whereas the two escapees accurately predicted the fate of the Hungarian Jews,[9] what they could not have foreseen was that their postwar memoirs and documented report would be kept from the Israeli Hebrew-reading public.[10]

In June 1998, fifty years after the escape, I took a poll of 594 students who were either in their third year of undergraduate studies or in their first year of graduate studies at the University of Haifa in Israel.[11] They were asked two questions: (1) "Did any Jew ever succeed in escaping from Auschwitz?" and (2) "Who are four Holocaust heroes that you are familiar with?" Ninety-eight percent of the respondents stated that no one had ever escaped from Auschwitz. The few who said they knew that some prisoners had escaped did not know any of their names. The students (half of them prospective teachers) were more knowledgeable about the second question and named Hanna Szenes, Anne Frank, Yanush Korczak, and Mordechai Anilewicz as among their Holocaust heroes. Some also named Oskar Schindler, the recent extracurricular addition from Hollywood.[12]

A few students might have heard about the escape through literature courses discussing the Hebrew version of Rolf Hochhuth's play *The Deputy*.[13] In it, Pope Pius XII is accused of callously watching the slaughter without extending a hand to help Jews. The play concerns three exemplary individuals who dared to break the secrecy of the Final Solution: Kurt Gerstein, a Nazi Waffen SS officer who in 1942 tried to inform the world about the horrors in Auschwitz, and Rudolf Vrba and Alfred Wetzler, who escaped in April 1944 in order to tell the world about the Auschwitz death factory. In the play, none of the three was believed. Yet, the lesson of Hochhuth's play, as well as the general Holocaust lesson taught to my university students, often seems to have been coupled with three predominant narratives: most Jewish victims went "like sheep to the slaughter"; a few succeeded in redeeming Jewish honor by resisting in the Warsaw Ghetto or fighting as partisans; and the world remained silent.[14]

Although I am a native Israeli who graduated from a prestigious private high school, I had never heard about the escape from Auschwitz at the numerous Holocaust ceremonies I attended. Nor had I ever read about it in any detail in any of the Hebrew Holocaust textbooks at school in my own time or in those given to my three children.[15] I became acquainted with this event during my adult life, through the non-Israeli "foreign" filmmaker Claude Lanzmann, who considered Vrba's testimony central to the understanding of the Holocaust in his 1987 movie *Shoah*.[16] The "presence" of the "absence" of the escape from Auschwitz in Israeli historiography on the one hand and the moral visibility and sanctity of Auschwitz in the country's hegemonic narrative on the other remained a puzzle for me,[17] and my desire to gain firsthand knowledge of the escape stayed with me for many years.

A breakthrough came in 1994, during a stay at the University of British Columbia. It transpired that I did not have to travel far to accomplish my goal: The Auschwitz escapee in Lanzmann's documentary was my neighbor at the same university, where he worked as Associate Professor of Pharmacology in the Faculty of Medicine. My meeting with him, and my subsequent reading of his book in English, led me to modify my original research question. I was no longer concerned with probing the escape from Auschwitz: I was able to learn about this in vivid detail by reading Vrba's memoirs, which were originally published in London in 1963 and had come out a year later in the United States.[18] But a new and more pressing research question now formed in my mind: Why, fifty years after the Holocaust, should the unique actions and memoirs of the Auschwitz escapees have remained completely unfamiliar to the average Hebrew reader?[19]

Meanwhile, elsewhere in Israel, Yehoshua Ben Ami, although having an entirely different history from mine and unknown to me, was asking himself the same questions. Yehoshua was twenty years old when his sisters and parents were sent to Auschwitz from Hungary. After escaping from a labor camp, he joined the underground. None of his family returned after the war. He immigrated to Israel, where he married Irka, an Auschwitz survivor. He studied and began working as a school counselor. The question of whether there had been any way his family could have been saved gave Yehoshua no peace. Upon his retirement he started searching for an answer. He came across Vrba's book in English, and from this point on he started making extraordinary efforts to track down the author who proved hesitant to establishing contact with an unknown Israeli. Finally, in 1994 (and with Vrba's permission), he began to translate the book into Hebrew. Yehoshua and I were not acquainted. We both had come to know Vrba independently, but now we joined forces to have Vrba's book published in Hebrew. Each of us felt that we should have heard about the escape from Auschwitz long before and found it imperative to pass it on to the younger generations of Hebrew readers. But what we had not taken into account was that no publishing house, including Yad Vashem, would show any interest at all. We were reminded of the case of Hannah Arendt, the well-known German-Jewish philosopher who in 1961 was sent by the *New Yorker* to cover the Eichmann trial in Jerusalem. Her book *Eichmann in Jerusalem: A Report on the Banality of Evil*,[20] first published in 1963, remained inaccessible to the average Hebrew reader for as long as Vrba's book, also published in 1963.[21]

Without Vrba's knowledge, I made it my mission to break a thirty-five–year silence. I at once approached Professor Aaron Ben Ze'ev, who, as dean of research at the time, was in charge of Haifa University Press. Although he, too, was unfamiliar with the story, his training in philosophy did much to help us overcome the hurdle of getting Vrba's book published in Hebrew. But a long battle awaited us in the university's senate: "If he was indeed a hero," I was repeatedly approached by some senate members who were ignorant about the case, "why wasn't he awarded this status long ago by Yad Vashem, the Holocaust Martyrs' and Heroes' Remembrance Authority, whose Holocaust scholars are among those who shape the Holocaust studies in Israel?"

Following the publication of his book in Hebrew, the senate of Haifa University, in June 1998, awarded Dr. Vrba an honorary doctorate in recognition of his heroic escape from Auschwitz and his contribution to Holocaust education. The award ceremony was planned to coincide with the first publication of the book in Hebrew by the Haifa University Press, allowing the author to sign copies for those present. To my surprise, even at this undeniably historic moment, some Israeli scholars, even within my own university, made a desperate last-minute attempt to belittle the hero and his memoirs. This included letters of defamation to the press (the first signed anonymously by "Four Historians"[22]), and a number of bizarre phone calls to my home and even to the university president's office.

No less interesting was the position of "intellectual bystanders" taken up by the Holocaust historians' establishment in Israel: not one of them publicly protested the campaign against Vrba. It was here that Michael Walzer's profound question crept into my mind: "What is the use, after all, of a silent intellectual"?[23]

But other voices were raised as well. Hanna Horovitz, for example, a retired history teacher living near Jerusalem, wrote to the daily newspaper *Ha'aretz;* "How is it possible that such a book was not published by the University History Department? . . . Am I to believe that this is accidental?"[24]

Why is it, in fact, that Vrba's book and the voice of its author reached the Israeli audience only thirty-five years after its original publication and at the initiative of two individuals whose profession is education, not history?

My primary aim in this book is to rename Vrba in the Israeli "reality." As Wyschnogrod tells us: "Naming the historical object is a response to the other's mortality: to name is to make us forget the fact of death, to write over it."[25] In what follows then, I delve into the mystery of Vrba's disappearance not only from Auschwitz but also from the Israeli textbooks and the Israeli Holocaust narrative.

This book is not a balanced one: No one should expect that suppressors and suppressed will be given equal weight. I have my own absences—I was not there and I can neither a priori nor a posteriori decide who was right and who was wrong. Inevitably, what I present here is my way of understanding the "presence" of the "absence" of Vrba's tale and the linkage between historical "truth" and the power of naming.

PART ONE

Between Auschwitz and Manhattan: Vrba Meets Arendt

On September 8, 1963, parts of Hannah Arendt's report on Eichmann's trial in Jerusalem appeared in the English Sunday newspaper the *Observer*, conveying to her readers what she saw as the lessons the trial transmitted: "The trial was supposed to show them [the younger generation] . . . how the Jews had degenerated until they went to their death like sheep."

Arendt believed she was merely reporting what she witnessed in the trial: perpetrators, bystanders, and victims, all of whom were normal human beings.[1] She saw the Holocaust as a phenomenon that had been perpetrated on our planet by "ordinary people,"[2] not even by a particular group of "ordinary Germans,"[3] let alone by monsters. Arendt could see other potential Eichmanns in future genocides and totalitarian regimes, something later social psychologists would corroborate.[4] She feared that human banality had become the instrument of the inhuman and based her conceptualization on Raul Hilberg's 1961 monumental study of the destruction of the European Jewry.[5]

Arendt questioned the obsession displayed at the trial with the Warsaw ghetto uprising, which was less connected to the Eichmann trial than to the question of the wartime Jewish councils, known by the German pejorative Judenrate (s., Judenrat).[6] Hoping to avert the draconically anti-Jewish measures, the elected, self-chosen or directly imposed but always German-approved Jewish councils often lulled the masses into a false sense of security by keeping them in the dark regarding the real intention of the deportations. To achieve this, the Judenrate were presented with baits for collaborating, which for many would prove hard to resist: some amount of knowledge regarding the deportations and their destination, authority to compile the lists for "resettlement" of the Jews, and the ability to protect their families and close friends from deportations. Under admittedly impossible conditions, Judenrate activities were not without instances of protectionism, favoritism, and misuse of positions of public trust for personal advantage—all of which naturally resulted in bitter accusations leveled against them by the community. Not without reason, Arendt saw this scenario as "undoubtedly the darkest chapter of the whole dark story."[7]

And if resistance was the issue, Arendt argued, then it was imperative to study the connection between the functioning of the wartime Jewish leaders and the lack of Jewish opposition or to what extent the Jewish leaders might have contributed to the "sheep-to-the-slaughter" state of mind.[8] It certainly ought to have interested the prosecutor, who relentlessly kept asking the witnesses: Why did you not resist?

On September 15, 1963, a week after the publication of Arendt's thesis in the *Observer*, Jacob Talmon, a Hebrew University history professor who at the time was a visiting fellow at Oxford, responded:

> *Miss Arendt's* dissertation on Jewish "co-operation" is a display of atrocious bad taste. If that "collaboration" was such a very significant fact, all one can do is to hang one's head in silent shame and grief, while the courts do their job, and not gloat over it. But the whole argument is a piece of inflated nonsense. Anyone with the slightest knowledge of Jewish history knows that whenever and wherever a few Jews found themselves together their first reflex was to get organized, especially in an hour of trial.
>
> *Miss Arendt* does not accuse even the most ambitious of the Jewish "collaborationists" of deliberate treason. She condemns them for letting themselves be duped out of a lack of that insight into the nature of to-

talitarianism which has been vouched to her—and only to her—*in her Manhattan apartment Post Factum.* . . .

I was told of inmates of Auschwitz who while observing everyday the smoke from the gas chambers would still not believe the truth. Gradually and systematically the Nazis took away from the Jews not only the power to resist but even the will to live, and when the Judenrat grasped what the real aim of the Nazis was they were no more than helpless and benumbed hostages.

In the end, they all went down to a man to death with their brethren. Judenrat or no Judenrat, it would not have made the slightest difference in face of the unshakable resolve to track down and to send to the gas chambers the last Jewish baby of men like Eichmann—a "banal" type on whom *Miss Arendt* expends all those philosophical acrobatics and psychological profundities. . . .[9]

Talmon was quick to sign the letter "Professor of Modern History, Hebrew University, Jerusalem, and Visiting Fellow, St. Catherine's College, Oxford." He denied Dr. Arendt her own academic title, referring to her as "Miss" and questioning the credentials of this brilliant American political philosopher.

On September 22, 1963, Vrba, who was living in England at the time of the trial, wrote to the *Observer:*

As a Jewish inmate of Auschwitz from June 1942 until April 1944, it was not without amazement that I read last Sunday's letter from J. L. Talmon, Professor of Modern History, Hebrew University, Jerusalem. Professor Talmon asserts that "*the Nazis took away from the Jews the power to resist.*" Saying [this] he is besmirching the memory of those dead Jews, who not only in Warsaw but even in Auschwitz formed an underground movement together with other, non-Jewish prisoners and tried to fight from Auschwitz the Nazi death machinery, although it was not on equal terms they had to fight once they had been tricked into Auschwitz. Most Jews believed the Nazis when they said they were deporting the Jews to labor camps. And they thought that labor camps would be better than pogroms against their children in their homes all over Europe. Therefore, they went voluntarily to the new "reservations" in the "east," but when they arrived they were suddenly in the water-tight extermination factories and they could do nothing but die, whether they realized what was to happen to them or not.

Therefore the leaders of the underground in Auschwitz decided to send a warning to the Zionist leaders. Our underground leaders in Auschwitz cannot be blamed for the fact that most of the attempts to es-cape from Auschwitz and deliver the message failed. One of these lead-ers, Ernst Burger, from Vienna (who, incidentally, was not a Jew) ended with others on the gallows of Auschwitz for attempting to escape and to inform the world.

With my friend Fred Wetzler from Slovakia, I managed to escape from Auschwitz on April 7, 1944, and we headed straight for the Zion-ist leaders. In April 1944, we handed to a high representative of the Zion-ist movement, Dr. Oskar Neumann, a sixty-page detailed report on the fact that extermination of 1,760,000 Jews had taken place in Auschwitz and that preparations were complete for the annihilation of one million Jewish Hungarians during the very next weeks. Did the Judenrat (or the Judenverrat) in Hungary tell their Jews what was awaiting them? No, they remained silent and for this silence some of their leaders—for in-stance Dr. R. Kasztner—bartered their own lives and the lives of 1684 other "prominent" Jews directly from Eichmann. They were not "help-less and benumbed hostages" but clever diplomats who knew what their silence was worth. The 1684 Jews whom they bought from Eichmann included not only various prominent Zionists, not only relatives of Kasztner, etc., but also such Jews who were able to pay with millions, like the family of Manfred Weiss. At the same time they silently watched as more than 400,000 Hungarian Jews, unaware of their fate, were tricked into Auschwitz, where thousands of their children were not even gassed but merely thrown into the pyre alive.

Professor Talmon says that "they all went down to a man to death with their brethren, Judenrat or no Judenrat." Is he not aware that, for instance, Dr. Kasztner and his family were honored members of an of-ficial Zionistic group in Israel until somebody on a dark night in 1957 shot Kasztner in the streets of Tel Aviv? Is he not aware that they were saved with the help of Eichmann and his deputy (Wisliceny)? Professor Talmon considers that "Miss Arendt's dissertation on Jewish co-operation is a display of atrocious bad taste" and that "if that 'collaboration' was such a very significant fact, all one can do is to hang one's head in silent shame and grief." Now Professor Talmon is an historian, and he should understand that if we ponder and speak about the past it is because we think about the future. This historical phenomenon has to be faced if we are to understand mankind.

    Rudolf Vrba
    Sutton, Surrey

    This exchange of letters is not found in Israeli Hebrew history textbooks. Nor do we find the fact that the Vrba-Wetzler report was submitted in evidence as documents under NG-2061nt at the Nuremberg trials. Vrba was not invited to testify at the Eichmann trial in Jerusalem. The court's position in the latter case is quite interesting if we consider that actually 56 of the 121 prosecution witnesses whose testimony dominated the trial were not concerned with Eichmann, who was the accused.[10] We know that at least one judge, Halevi, voted in favor of bringing Vrba to testify. This proposal was rejected by the other two judges. The attorney general, Gideon Hausner, argued that the government could not cover the travel expenses for its witnesses.[11] More than thirty-five years later, on the eve of Vrba's visit to Israel, a prominent Israeli Holocaust historian explained to me that "Vrba was probably not invited since the state of Israel had no money to sponsor the flight from Vancouver, Canada." But Vrba was then living in London and larger sums were spent bringing in witnesses from more distant places. His whereabouts was known to the Slovak community in Israel, who, like other survivors, tried to affect the selection of the witnesses from their community and eventually the nature of the trial.[12] Vrba ended up giving a deposition against Eichmann at the Israeli embassy in London. The court appeared content with data "that reveal what was known" and not necessarily with those voices that reveal "what could be known."[13] It is this tension—among the voices of the informants, the informed, and the uninformed—that lies at the heart of this book.

ONE

THE INFORMANTS

The truth about Auschwitz was the best-kept secret of the architects of the Final Solution, guarded from discovery by more than two thousand SS personnel, two hundred vicious dogs, two lines of electrified fences, and a terrorized, fearful Polish population living around the camp.[1] The secrecy was further preserved by limiting and restricting the prisoners' movements inside the camp, particularly those of Jews.

Throughout the five years of the camp's existence there were hundreds of attempts by prisoners to escape. Seventy-six of these were by Jews. Of these only five succeeded in getting away to reveal the secrets of Auschwitz and to survive the war to tell their stories.[2]

On April 5, 1944, a Jewish inmate named Ziegfried Lederer fled, dressed in an SS uniform, with the help of an SS guard named Viktor Pestek. Pestek is known to have fallen in love with a Jewish girl from the Czech "family camp," Renée Neumann, whom he wanted to rescue and even marry.[3] Built by the Nazis in September 1943 within Auschwitz-Birkenau, the family camp was intended to deceive the outside world. Its inmates were kept intact as families and were even allowed to send postcards and to receive food parcels from the International Red Cross. Like other inmates in the family camp, Renée did not know that within a few months, her entire transport would be gassed. She refused to leave the camp without her mother.

In his search for another prisoner to serve as an escape partner, Pestek broached the idea to Vrba and Wetzler. These experienced prisoners, who had witnessed numerous incidents of betrayal, refused to believe that a Nazi would want to help a single Jew escape from Auschwitz. Pestek then approached Lederer, a former Czech army officer, who had arrived at Auschwitz on December 19, 1943, from Theresienstadt.[4] In return for his help in being smuggled out, Lederer could offer Pestek the aid of his friends in Bohemia. The decision of this ethnic German from Bukovina (Romania) and SS member to help a Jew escape may have been self-serving in other ways as well. In March 1944, when Romania was invaded by the advancing Russians, Pestek probably realized that he would not be able to return home without a solid testimony to his anti-Nazi activity. On April 5, the disguised Lederer left Auschwitz-Birkenau accompanied by Pestek. They traveled by train to Prague, successfully passing through border controls. Pestek returned to Auschwitz, hoping to organize another escape for Renée and her mother. But he was identified, arrested, and subjected to savage interrogation by the SS. He was executed on October 8, 1944.

After his escape, Lederer risked his life several times in sneaking into the Theresienstadt ghetto to warn the Jews about the fate that was awaiting them in Auschwitz. But the ghetto inmates were not willing to listen to his warning: Many of them had just received from Auschwitz (postdated) postcards from their (already gassed) relatives at the family camp.

Researchers suspect that Lederer's message on Auschwitz was blocked by a central member of the ghetto's Jewish Council, Dr. Leo Baeck, the former chief rabbi of Germany, who believed that given the "certainty" of their approaching death, it was better not to inform the potential victims.[5]

Disappointed by the lack of response, Lederer desperately tried to inform the outside world by means of letters to the Red Cross in Switzerland. He later joined the Czech partisans and fought with them until the end of the war. After the war he stayed in Czechoslovakia, where he died on April 5, 1972, bitter and forgotten.[6] Not a single notice appeared in the Czech media, let alone in Israel.

On April 7, 1944, two days after Lederer escaped, two other inmates, Vrba and Wetzler, followed. Among attempts to break down the wall of silence around the Auschwitz secrets, historians have no doubt that this was by far the most important escape.[7]

Born as Walter Rosenberg in Topolcany, Czechoslovakia, in 1924, Vrba was expelled in 1939 from the high school (gymnasium) of Bratislava at the age of fifteen, under the Slovak state's version of the anti-Jewish Nuremberg laws. Early in March 1942, in rebellion against the deportation laws, Vrba ripped the yellow Star of David off his clothes and left his Czechoslovakian home in a taxi, heading for England via Hungary. Later intercepted and beaten by frontier guards, he was first sent to the Novaky transition camp in Slovakia where he tried to escape but again was caught and beaten.[8] On June 14, 1942, he was sent to the Majdanek concentration camp and two weeks later, on June 30, to Auschwitz. After six months in Auschwitz, he was transferred to Birkenau (Auschwitz II) and had the number 44070 tattooed on his arm. From August 1942 until June 1943 Vrba was assigned (both in Auschwitz and in Birkenau) to work in the special slave labor unit that handled the property of those who had already been gassed. In camp slang, the unit was known as "Canada" because of the food and the gold and other precious materials that the Germans confiscated from the luggage of the incoming resettlement deportees. The Auschwitz treasures from "Canada" were packaged for Germany, and the gold was quickly melted into ingots and deposited in the Reichsbank.

Registered as number 29162, Alfred Wetzler was taken to Birkenau and put in the men's camp. He was later moved to the Birkenau mortuary, where he remained, except for a short time in the spring of 1942 when he was in the main camp, Auschwitz. His task was to record the numbers of prisoners who died within the camp other than by gassing, and the amount of gold teeth extracted from them.

A major aspect of Vrba's duties in "Canada" during 1942–1943 was to be present at the arrival of most transports of deportees and to sort the belongings of the gassed victims. From this vantage point Vrba was able to assess how much deportees knew about Auschwitz when they entered the camp. As he quickly determined, prospective victims were totally ignorant about what was in store for them: Their luggage contained clothing for all seasons and basic utensils, a clear sign of their naive preparation for a new life in the area of "resettlement" in the East. In the summer of 1943, Vrba improved his position for collecting information when he was appointed registrar (*Block Schreiber*) in the quarantine camp for men (Birkenau, sector B IIa). From his barrack he could observe how all arriving deportees destined to be gassed were transported on trucks from the ramp to the gas chambers in Birkenau. He was able not only to estimate the number of Jews arriving daily at the death factory but also to calculate accurately that on average about 10 percent of each incoming transport were exempted from gassing for the purpose of slave labor.

At the beginning of 1944, Vrba noticed that preparations were underway for an additional railway line, which seemed aimed at increasing the efficiency of the killing process by having the prospective victims arrive directly at the gas chambers. This plan was confirmed on January 15, 1944, by the remarks of a German kapo who was connected with the building of the extended railway and had knowledge of the expected transports of Jews. Vrba had no doubt about the identity of the new victims, who in the SS camp language were called "Hungarian salami." Transports from different countries, Vrba would later explain, were characterized by certain long-lasting provisions packed in their luggage (for the final journey into the unknown), which reflected the typical foodstuffs still available in various countries of German-occupied Europe. This food—together with all other luggage—was taken from the new arrivals immediately and was sent to the "Canada" stores, whence perishables as well as tinned foods found their way to the SS officers' mess. As Vrba subsequently wrote, "When a series of transports of Jews from the Netherlands arrived, cheeses enriched the wartime rations. It was sardines when series of transports of French Jews arrived, Chalva and olives when transports of Jews from Greece reached the camp, and now the SS were talking of 'Hungarian salami', a well-known Hungarian provision suitable for taking along on a long journey."[9]

For almost two years he had thought of escape, at first selfishly, because he had merely wanted his freedom, but now, "I had an imperative reason. It was no longer a question of reporting a crime, but of pre-

venting one."[10] Yet, it required a trustworthy escape partner and mas-
terly planning. Vrba wasted no time. He approached Alfred Wetzler.
"He was from my home town in Trnava, and, although I had never spo-
ken to him for he was six years older than I was, I had always admired
him, if only for his casual bohemian manner and his easy way with
girls."[11] Of all six hundred deportees from Trnava in 1942, Vrba and
Wetzler were the only ones still alive.

The would-be escapees considered various scenarios. They knew
that after they were missed, the prison guards would stay on duty for
three days and nights while the troops and dogs combed the stretch of
land that lay between the inner and outer perimeters of the camp. If
they were not recaptured in that time, the Germans would presume
that they had escaped beyond the confines of the camp and turn the
search over to the police apparatus. Vrba concluded: "It was clear to me
that a man who could remain hidden beyond the inner perimeter for
three days and nights had a reasonable chance. It was not so clear to me,
however, how this could be accomplished, and therefore I began what
was to be my first scientific study: the technique of escape. I began to
study every unsuccessful escape attempt, to analyze its flaws and to
correct them."[12]

Paradoxically, it was the Nazis' preparations for the influx of Hungarians that made it possible for Vrba and Wetzler to escape.[13] A large
pile of lumber assembled to build an extension of the Birkenau camp
offered a possible hiding place. On Friday, April 7, 1944, at 2 P.M. (the
eve of Passover), Vrba and Wetzler sneaked into a previously used
hideout located in an area known as Mexico, which was being prepared to house the expected Hungarian Jews selected for slave labor,
after they had first sprinkled it with gasoline-soaked tobacco to prevent the dogs from sniffing them out. They hid there for three nights,
until the camp authorities assumed that the two men had already got-
ten beyond the outer perimeter. When the cordon of SS guards, which
had surrounded that perimeter, was withdrawn, Vrba and Wetzler were
ready to sneak out.[14]

Because of impenetrable fog, however, they were forced to stay
within the camp and managed to sneak out only on May 11 at 5 A.M.,

less than an hour before the towers of the outer perimeter were re-manned. Vrba had a stolen watch and could also rely on his memory of a fragment of a map he had briefly glimpsed in a children's atlas found in a suitcase in "Canada." He learned that Auschwitz was on the River Sola and that to follow the river upstream was the shortest route to the border of Slovakia.

Vrba and Wetzler knew one thing for certain: As shaven-headed in-mates, clad in striped pajamas and with numbers tattooed on their arms, there was no point in relying on any help in the world outside Auschwitz. "At the moment of our escape," explains Vrba, "all connec-tions with whatever friends and social contacts we had in Auschwitz were severed, and we had absolutely no connection waiting for us out-side the death camp where we had spent the past two years: We were *de facto* written off by the world from the moment we were loaded into a deportation train in the spring of 1942. To start with, we had to step into a complete 'social vacuum' outside of Auschwitz. The only ad-ministrative evidence of our existence was an international warrant about us, issued telegraphically and distributed to all stations of the Gestapo. . . ."[15] The warrant was also telegraphed to all stations of the Kripo (Criminal Police), the SD (Sicherheitsdients, Security Service), and the Grepo (Grenzpolizei, Border Police) and even reached the desk of Himmler.[16] Some historians speculate that Eichmann was among the informed as well.[17]

With the exception of this warrant, there was no sign that anyone expected Vrba and Wetzler in the outside world. The escapees were forced to bank on a certain amount of luck. Particularly as Jews they had to dismiss any thought of being assisted by any organization of the Polish population. Fifty years later, Polish historiography would argue that the escape was possible "thanks to the local people's stance and also that of the Polish underground operating near the camp, which con-centrated its efforts on helping prisoners. Camp escapees were not left to their own decisions and luck."[18]

On April 21, 1944, after eleven days of a dangerous journey, Vrba and Wetzler came upon a farmer plowing his fields. He answered their question in Slovak. It was then that they first realized they had crossed the border into their home country. Twenty-three years later, some Israeli Holocaust historians try to claim the escape as a collective (and eventually Zionist) enterprise: "The fugitives had no inkling and are perhaps to this day ignorant of the fact that the help they got was probably the first organized aid of Jewish organizations in Slovakia. . . . this [Zionist] organization was able by means of money from abroad to get the peasants to furnish help to Jewish fugitives."[19]

It was only after reaching the town of Cadca in Slovakia, however, that the escapees initiated a first contact with a formal Jewish organization. They learned about this possibility from a Dr. Pollack, whom Vrba knew from his first imprisonment in Novaky. Dr. Pollack, the escapees found out, was one of many Slovak Jewish doctors who had been exempted from "resettlement" in order to serve the farmers who otherwise would have been left without medical services. Asking to talk privately with him about the "male's disease," the unidentifiable Vrba quickly revealed his Auschwitz background and mission and asked Dr. Pollack for help in establishing contact with the available Slovak Jewish leaders. Dr. Pollack arranged for the Slovak Jewish Council to send representatives from their headquarters in Bratislava to the nearby town of Zilina to meet the escapees the following day. Vrba left Dr. Pollack's office with a bandage on his foot to counter any possible suspicions. But he left behind an emotionally wounded Jewish physician, who, until that moment, had hoped that his family was still alive in the new "resettlement" area to which they had been sent.

The meeting in Zilina on April 24 had a profound effect on the remnant of the Slovak Jewish Council, which now called itself the "Working Group" and considered itself to be an underground body. After Leo Baeck, they would be the first Jewish leaders to meet Jewish Auschwitz escapees and receive from them inside details about the secret death factory there. Their head, Dr. Oskar Neumann, a skillful German-speaking lawyer, decided to record the escapees' account in the most meticulous and professionally legal manner: Vrba and Wetzler were put into separate rooms, where for three days each dictated his account to Dr. Neumann's aide, Oscar Krasniansky, an engineer who was also a good stenographer. Neumann recalled: "The moment the group in Bratislava was informed about the 'find' it sent one of its faithful workers to write down from the [two] chaps all they had to tell. This task was performed by the messenger in the best possible way. . . . The testimony that he wrote, forty typewritten pages, was one of the most shocking documents the human ear could hear. . . . our people heard this story and they thought that they would go mad."[20]

By comparing the names provided by the two escapees with the old lists of deported Jews, the Slovak Jewish leaders could identify Vrba and Wetzler as well as test their knowledge. The escapees were cross-examined about their statements. The two transcripts (in the Slovak language) were immediately translated into German and then hastily collated into a single report. Vrba and Wetzler also produced a precise sketch of the camp layout from memory. Krasniansky then added a one-page introduction containing biographical notes on the anonymous escapees and vouching for the report's accuracy and authenticity. Vrba's signature, for example, had to be notarized by an adult since he was not yet twenty-one years old. All these procedures enhanced the validity of the account. Krasniansky also added a supplement in which he urged the Allies to destroy the crematoria and the railroad lines leading to Auschwitz.[21]

On June 6, 1944, the day of the Normandy landing, two other Jewish inmates, Czeslaw Mordowicz and Arnost Rosin, reached Slovakia after having escaped from Auschwitz on May 27. When these escapees heard about the Allied landing, they assumed that the war was over and decided to celebrate in the nearest bar, where they paid for their drinks with dollars they had smuggled from Auschwitz. They were promptly arrested and accused of violating currency laws. After eight days in prison and the payment of a fine by the Jewish Council of Slovakia, they were released. Three days later, on June 17, 1944, they were interviewed by Krasniansky.[22] The members of the Jewish Council soon realized that the new escapees, who had witnessed the gassing of the Hungarian Jews, wholly corroborated the shocking and factual account of Vrba and Wetzler. Mordowicz and Rosin confirmed that in the few days between May 15 and their escape on May 27, more than 100,000 Hungarian Jews had reached Birkenau where most had immediately been murdered in the gas chambers. In his postwar testimonies, Krasniansky claimed that Mordowicz's and Rosin's four-to-seven–page report on Auschwitz was attached to Vrba's and Wetzler's forty-page report, but there is no evidence of this.[23]

Under the German control, discovery of the escapees' arrival in Slovakia could have had profound consequences: If they or the report had been spotted, the members of the Working Group and their families would most likely have been liquidated immediately. Each escapee was provided with high-quality forged documents and money by the Slovak Jewish Council, which also arranged a hideout for them in a small Slovak town in the mountains (in Liptovsky Svaty Mikulas). When each pair of escapees parted from the Jewish leaders, they were assured that the report would be distributed without delay to all concerned parties at home and abroad.

In September 1944 Vrba joined the partisans, eventually to be awarded the highest medal for valor. Wetzler joined the partisans in February. While serving in his partisan unit, Vrba received a note from Rosin, who was still in Bratislava, in which he told him that Mordowicz was "very sick and was sent again to the sanatorium in which he stayed before." Mordowicz had been caught by the Nazis in Bratislava on September 9, 1944, and was returned to Auschwitz. On his arrival there, he was fortunately not recognized by the SS, and the registrar of prisoners quickly assigned him to another slave labor detail. One needs to remember that there were still deportation lists in September 1944 with the full knowledge of the Working Group. Although almost five months had elapsed since the secrets of Auschwitz had been revealed, Mordowicz discovered that not one of the passengers in the boxcar in which they were transported wanted to believe him; instead they beat him up.[24]

TWO

THE INFORMED

Once in the possession of the report, the Slovak Jewish leaders suddenly found the information they had sought all those years to be a mixed blessing: It shattered all illusions as to what was in store for those individuals they had been sending since 1942 for "resettlement." How should they deliver this alarming message to the West and to the potential victims, both at home (25,000) and in Hungary (800,000)?

The evidence as to what the informed leaders did with the Vrba-Wetzler report is complicated, fragmentary, and sometimes contradictory. It is not a simple task to follow the chain of events. It is even harder to fathom the motives and intentions of the acting figures. In the spring of 1944, all sides were racing against the clock: While the Germans were expanding their gas chambers, the remaining Jews and their leaders were trying to gain time in order to survive until the arrival of the rapidly advancing Russian troops.[1]

At the time of their deportation from Slovakia in 1942, Vrba and Wetzler were not fully aware of the role that the German-appointed Jewish councils were forced to play. The Slovak Judenrat (Ustredna Zidov [U.Z.]) was established as early as September 1940 at the instigation of Dieter Wisliceny, who had been appointed by Eichmann to be the Slovak government's advisor on Jewish affairs.[2] In 1940 the U.Z. was the only Jewish institution in existence, all others having been abolished. It was headed by a "starosta" (elder).[3] In 1941, under the leadership of Arpad Sebestyen, Dr. Oskar Neumann was in charge of the vocational training department, which eventually became the labor camp department.[4] Dr. Neumann was in office during the 1942 deportations of 58,000 (of 88,000) Slovak Jews to Auschwitz, Majdanek, and other "resettlement" camps. He later joined the underground body named the Working Group (Pracovna Skupina) that had been founded by Gizi Fleischmann, a Zionist activist who was the head of the immigration to Palestine section in the community's Jewish center. The spiritual guide in this project was Fleischmann's orthodox cousin, Rabbi Michael Dov Weissmandel, who, given the extreme nature of events, was willing to cooperate with a Zionist underground organization for the sake of rescuing all Jews.[5] In December 1943, Dr. Neumann was appointed acting "starosta" of the U.Z., and the Working Group thus became the official leadership of Slovak Jewry.[6] In April 1944, at the time of the escape from Auschwitz, he was the chairman of the Jewish Council in Slovakia, and it was under his aegis that the Vrba-Wetzler report was composed. Dr. Neumann served in this role until the fall of 1944 when the Jewish Center was abolished by the German army.

The deportations from Slovakia had started in March 26, 1942, with a transport of girls and women to Auschwitz.[7] In late June Rabbi Weissmandel came up with the idea of paying a ransom to Wisliceny, Eichmann's deputy in Slovakia, in exchange for a halt to the deportations. When the first wave of deportations ceased (and indeed there were none from October 1942 to the fall of 1944), Weissmandel and Fleischmann believed that this was the result of their bribe to Wisliceny. As a consequence of this naive assessment, the two activists grew bolder and submitted to Wisliceny a more daring proposal, their so-called Europe Plan. This called for the cessation of deportations from all parts of German-occupied Europe in exchange for foreign currency or goods amounting to two million dollars, which would be conveyed to the Germans by Jews in free countries.[8] They would soon advise the Hungarian Jewish leaders to follow in their footsteps in their attempt to halt the deportations.

Warnings could have been delivered to the uninformed masses via two leaders in Hungary. The first was Filip von Freudiger, a relative of Rabbi Weissmandel, who was the leader of the Budapest Orthodox Jewish community and with whom Weissmandel maintained frequent contact. The second was Dr. Rezsö Kasztner, a journalist and lawyer and also a daring Zionist activist, first in his hometown in Cluj, Transylvania, and, after its annexation by Hungary in 1940, in Budapest. Kasztner's job, which he shared with Joel Brand, was to help the Jewish refugees who were pouring into Hungary, a flow that swelled in March 1942, when Slovakia was chosen as the first country where the Final Solution was to be implemented. At the time of the escape of Vrba and Wetzler, Kasztner was the deputy chairman of the Rescue Committee in Budapest and a member of Mapai (Labor Party, the smallest faction in the Zionist movement in Hungary). Throughout the war he had maintained his connection with the Zionist members of the Working Group and habitually visited Bratislava.[9]

Counting on Weissmandel's spiritual guidance and widespread connections, Dr. Neumann decided to send him the Vrba-Wetzler report. Weissmandel immediately recognized the significance of the information it contained. He therefore sought to make the content known to his circle in the West, particularly in Switzerland but also in Hungary. For this purpose he had the report translated into Yiddish. Later he would ask to meet the escapees themselves.

Weissmandel was racing against time. He sent a warning note to his relatives in Hungary on May 10 or 11. This letter never reached its destination. On May 15, 1944, Weissmandel's plans for the dispatch of the Vrba-Wetzler report were interrupted by the large-scale deportations of the Hungarian Jews. The remaining Slovak Jews, Weissmandel included, witnessed these transport trains from Hungary to Auschwitz crossing through Slovakia. Weissmandel took this traffic as a sign that his warning had not reached Freudiger. Consequently, on May 16 or May 22 (both dates appear on the letter), he composed a letter to the Swiss Orthodox Jewish leaders for transmission to the United States. In this letter, which most likely was based on his knowledge of the Vrba-Wetzler report, he urged the Allies to bombard the railways lines between Kosice and Presov. Perhaps for safety reasons, Weissmandel did not mention the name Auschwitz.[10]

Whereas Freudiger, now a member of the Hungarian Judenrat, may have been informed of the content of the Vrba-Wetzler report *before* the deportations from Hungary started, the detailed document itself probably reached him only on June 10, 1944.[11] As soon as he had read it, Freudiger knew he had to flee. He managed to do so a month after the end of the deportations from Hungary. On August 9, he left for Bucharest with eighty members of his family. There he wrote a memorandum that reached the West, in which he made no mention of the Vrba-Wetzler report. In his postwar testimonies, Freudiger provided two different dates and versions of how he became aware of the Vrba-Wetzler report.[12]

In late April, aware of Kasztner's forthcoming regular visit to Bratislava, Krasniansky had quickly translated the German version of the original report into Hungarian. According to one of the (three) versions of Krasniansky's postwar testimony, he personally handed the translation to Kasztner toward the end of the month. According to Bauer, the report must have arrived in Budapest "perhaps through Kasztner at the end of April and have been handed over to the leading members of the Judenrat." But this transfer was not a promising one, as Bauer further explains: "abandoned by the government, handed over to the mercy of the SS, unaccustomed to and incapable of any illegal work, the [Hungarian] Judenrat obeyed the Nazis."[13]

Like Freudiger, Kasztner was convinced from reading the Vrba-Wetzler report that the entire Jewish community in Hungary was doomed to be liquidated. In his mind the only hope was to try to save the few, whether through bribery or an imaginative plan whereby the Hungarian Zionist leaders would offer their Jewish international connections for contact between the Allies and the Germans.[14] During May and June, Kasztner was involved in delicate negotiations with Eichmann regarding the release of 1684 prominent Jews, including 388 members of his family and friends from his hometown Cluj, who were eventually taken to Budapest. Under the aegis of Eichmann himself, Kasztner's train left Hungary on June 30. On July 8, it reached Bergen-Belsen. From there the travelers were taken in two batches, in August and December, to Switzerland.[15]

During his intense negotiation with the SS, Kasztner kept the Vrba-Wetzler report secret in order not to create panic among the potential deportees to Auschwitz. In his postwar memoirs Kasztner was quick to state that by the end of April he was fully aware of the implications of the term "Hungarian salami," a statement that suggests that he was cognizant of the Vrba–Wetzler report and the predictions of these escapees about the imminent fate of the Hungarian Jews.[16]

THOUGH the record is ambiguous as to the exact date the Vrba–Wetzler report was forwarded to the West and the representatives of the Christian Church, the evidence is clear that the members of the Working Group had been very creative in this regard. Shortly after the two sets of escapees arrived in Bratislava, Krasniansky arranged a secret meeting with a member of the Vatican, who had been temporarily posted to Bratislava, to have him question them personally and pass the report to the pope. On June 20 Vrba and Mordowicz met with Vatican legate Monsignor Mario Martilotti (whom they mistakenly thought was Burzio) at a remote Slovakian monastery. The meeting lasted for several hours. The papal diplomat promised to take their report back to Switzerland on the next day, and then to forward its ominous contents to his superiors in the Vatican. This he did, and on June 25, 1944, the pope issued an unprecedented appeal in an open telegram to the Hungarian Regent, Admiral Miklos Horthy, calling on him to "spare so many unfortunate people further sufferings," without explicitly mentioning Jews.[17]

The pope was not the only one whom the informed Slovak Jewish leaders aimed at warning. They also sent the Vrba–Wetzler report to the Zionist liaison committee in Istanbul and to the Zionist representative in Switzerland, Nathan Schwalb. Although he was active in encouraging resistance to the Nazis and was involved in numerous rescue efforts, some researchers argue that apparently Schwalb's primary interest in this instance was to prevent the Vrba–Wetzler report from being published so as not to disrupt Kasztner's negotiation with Eichmann.[18]

There is evidence that on June 10 the Vrba–Wetzler report reached the Czechoslovak embassy in Switzerland, together with the "Polish major's report," which was sent from the underground organization in Slovakia.[19] It is not clear how this report reached the members of the

Working Group.[20] It had been written by Jerzy Tabeau, a non-Jewish Polish medical student, who had been sent to Auschwitz on March 24, 1942, from Krakow and had escaped from Birkenau on November 19, 1943. Like Vrba, Tabeau wanted to get to London through Hungary. Yet, he reached Budapest on March 19, 1944, the exact day of the German invasion of Hungary. He managed to report to the Polish committee there, before quickly leaving Budapest and returning to Poland. There he wrote a detailed nineteen-page report on Auschwitz "of which three pages dealt entirely with the Jews. He, too, [like Vrba and Wetzler] gave one and a half million as the number of Jews gassed at Birkenau since the spring of 1942" until November 1943.[21] According to Henryk Swiebocki, it was the Polish underground that made sure that Tabeau's report was sent to Switzerland in June 1944.[22] Tabeau joined the partisans and fought until the liberation. After the war he continued his medical studies and eventually became a cardiologist in Krakow, unaware that his anonymous testimony had become "the Polish major's report."[23]

When the reports reached the Czechoslovak embassy in Bern on June 10, 1944, Dr. Jaromir Kopecky, the Geneva representative of the Czechoslovak government-in-exile, found the Vrba-Wetzler report of great interest; of all the information in it, the prospective fate of the inmates of the Czech "family camp" was the most pressing for Kopecky. On September 8, 1943, 2,293 men and 2,713 women, altogether 5,006 Czechoslovak Jews from Theresienstadt, had arrived there.[24] On March 3, 1944, more than a month before Vrba and Wetzler escaped, inmates of the family camp were told to write postcards, which they had to date March 25, 26, and 27, asking their relatives abroad to send them food parcels. On March 8, exactly six months after their arrival, the surviving 3,791 Jews of that September transport were gassed.

The second transport of another 2,473 Theresienstadt deportees (1,137 men and 1,336 women) had been added to the family camp on December 20, 1943. This brought the total to almost 7,500 people.

Dr. Kopecky realized that he had to act at once if he wanted to avert the murder of these Czech citizens.[25]

Because of its high level of credibility, Kopecky used the Vrba-Wetzler report as grounds for an alarming telegram in which he stated, among other things:

> According [to the] report made by two Slovakian Jews who escaped from Birkenau to Bratislava and whose reliability is assured by Jewish leaders there, 3000 Czechoslovakian Jews who were brought from Terezin to Birkenau on December 20, 1943 . . . will be gassed after six months' quarantine on about June 20, 1944. Appealing most urgently that this news may be broadcast immediately through the BBC and American radio in order to prevent at the last moment this new massacre. . . . Please issue without delay most impressive warning to German butchers who [are] directing slaughters [in] Upper Silesia. Do not mention Bratislava as source. Further reports following. Please inform immediately also the Czechoslovakian government.[26]

The message reached the British Legation in Bern, the World Jewish Congress in Geneva, and Allen Dulles, head of United States intelligence in Switzerland; Dulles conveyed it to the War Refugee Board representative in Bern, Roswell McClelland, who received it on June 16. On June 18, it was at last broadcast by the BBC. The reliability of the report seemed to convince even the Swiss censor, who for the first time allowed such reports to be printed, an action that resulted in no fewer than 383 articles and reprints in the following eighteen days in the Swiss press.[27] It was only in November 1944, after the gas chambers at Birkenau had almost ceased to function, that the full texts of the Vrba-Wetzler report, the Mordowicz-Rosin report, and the Polish major's report actually reached the War Refugee Board in Washington, D.C.[28]

The Vrba-Wetzler report may be credited with making three major breakthroughs. First, before its arrival, the Allies thought that Auschwitz was a huge labor concentration camp mainly for Poles. Second, unlike previous Polish reports, it was the first detailed and reliable report. Third, it shook Swiss (pro-German) neutrality and jolted the Swiss into undertaking wide publication of the German mass killing at Auschwitz.[29]

Among those who were fully informed about the Vrba-Wetzler report in London but kept it secret was Joseph Korbel, a Czechoslovak diplomat and the father of the future U.S. secretary of state under President Clinton, Madeleine Albright. Madeleine was nearly two years old when her parents whisked her out of Czechoslovakia in March 1939, less than two weeks after the start of the Nazi occupation, giving up the life they had been living of a prominent Czech diplomatic family and escaping to London. There, Joseph Korbel converted to Christianity and joined Benes' government in exile that was to become the focal point of Czech resistance to the Nazis. As the head of its information department, Korbel received the information about the Vrba-Wetzler report on June 19. Though he himself had relatives in the Auschwitz-Birkenau family camp, he seems to have dissociated himself from its content. Michael Dobbs, Albright's biographer, hypothesizes that the reason may have been that acknowledging familiarity with the horrors of the report would have led Korbel to face the question "why are you concerned [about your relatives]?" and he would have to admit, "They are Jews." But that he was not prepared to say.[30]

It was only during the second half of June, a month and a half after the Hungarian Jewish leaders had become informed and when the deportations were in full swing (and already 300,000 Jews had been gassed), that they started disseminating copies of the report to the Hungarian authorities and to the Swiss representatives.[31] It was Miklos (Moshe) Krausz, the executive secretary of the Budapest branch of the Palestine Office and a bitter rival of Kasztner, who took the initiative. Krausz, like Kasztner, was exempted from the anti-Jewish laws (for example, wearing the yellow star) and had retained his freedom of movement. He further had the privilege of finding refuge in the Swiss Legation in Budapest. His contact with representatives of neutral countries helped him to save Jews in various ways. On June 18, Krausz happened to receive the Vrba-Wetzler report from Josef Reisner, a clerk in the Turkish Legation.[32] It is possible that the copy that reached Reisner and Krausz was one of the several that Vrba's friend, Josef Weiss, then an employee of the Ministry of Health in Bratislava, helped to disseminate.[33] The following day Krausz forwarded an abbreviated version of the Vrba-Wetzler report to Geneva with the help of Florian Manoliu, a member of the Romanian Legation in Bern, who delivered it to George Mandel-Mantello, a Jewish businessman serving as the first secretary of the El Salvador consulate general in Geneva. Mandel-Mantello disseminated the report further to the media and also passed it on to Walter Garrett, a chief correspondent of the British Exchange Press in Zurich, whose Hungarian-speaking secretary translated the documents from Hungarian into English and immediately informed his London office.[34] On June 19, a detailed summary of the Vrba-Wetzler report was sent by Richard Lichtheim of the Jewish Agency's Geneva office to the Jewish Agency leadership in Jerusalem. There is some evidence that on receiving this information, the Jewish Agency leadership promptly launched a concerted lobbying effort to persuade the Allies to bomb Auschwitz.[35]

One of the copies of the original German version of the Vrba-Wetzler report reached Geza Soos, head of a relatively small resistance group called the Hungarian Independent Movement. Soos handed his copy for translation and duplication to the Reverend Jozsef Elias, the head of the Good Shepherd Mission, perhaps during the first few days of May. His secretary, Maria Szekely, translated the report into Hungarian and English in six copies and distributed them to the top leaders of the Christian churches and the Hungarian state shortly before the start of the mass deportations in the middle of May.[36]

The recurring need for translation of the Vrba-Wetzler report helps us not only to locate it historically but also to detect the psychological impact it had on its various readers and the action plans they subsequently made. The need of the Hungarian underground to translate the report from German suggests that it was not sent in this case by the Working Group, as Krasniansky had already translated it into Hungarian two weeks before. Bauer argues that the copy that was supposedly given to Otto Komoly, the leader of the Zionist group in Budapest, seems not to have come from the Working Group either since Komoly's daughter testified that she translated the protocols from German into Hungarian for her father and it was handed to him on June 14, 1944.[37]

Among the Hungarians who received a copy of the Vrba-Wetzler report were Horthy's daughter-in-law, cardinals in the Catholic Church, Lutheran bishops, and Erno Peto, a prominent Judenrat member. Peto claimed that he gave the Hungarian translation to Horthy's son and some other officials. But why would Hungarian dignitaries need a translated version of the Vrba-Wetzler report as they were educated in the Austro-Hungarian monarchy and could read the German text of the report just as well?

The Vrba-Wetzler report had an immediate impact.[38] The publication of portions of the report in the Swiss press in the final days of June and by the Western Allies shortly afterward produced a spontaneous international denunciation, which led to protests from the pope, the U.S. Secretary of State Cordell Hull, British Foreign Secretary Anthony Eden, the International Red Cross, and the king of Sweden, amounting to a "bombardment of Horthy's conscience."

On July 5, Eden stated that the BBC would be employed to warn the Hungarian leaders. On July 7, 1944, Admiral Miklos Horthy ordered a halt to the deportations from Hungary, which became effective only on July 9.[39] Almost 200,000 Jews in Budapest were thus saved from deportation. They were subsequently to be harassed by members of the Arrow Cross (Nyilas) movement, whose anti-Semitic butchery, however, was no match for German efficiency: They managed to kill approximately 50,000 Jews during their three months of fearsome rule, a small number compared with the approximately 437,000 Hungarian Jews smoothly liquidated by the Germans in less than eight weeks in the spring of 1944.

Was there a way to intervene before Horthy stopped the deportations? Bauer is skeptical: "How else could he [Kasztner] have warned the Jews in Hungary? By radio? Through the press? By giving lectures? These questions are so ridiculous that they do not deserve an answer." Horthy remained the key figure in this drama "But Horthy kept silent"—*until* he was faced with the specific details of the Vrba-Wetzler report. As Bauer puts it: "through the protocols he must have learned details about what was already known in general—that with his connivance a mass murder was being committed against Hungarian citizens."[40]

Considering that Admiral Horthy's position was what one might call armchair anti-Semitism,[41] and given the political impact of the reports sent to the West from Bratislava, one can only wonder how many more Jewish lives could have been saved had Horthy read the Vrba-Wetzler report earlier. As Bauer notes, "Clearly, if Horthy stopped the deportations in early July, he could have stopped them earlier as well. There were no German troops of consequence in Budapest, and the Germans were otherwise occupied. Rescue was possible, and it seems that had information about Auschwitz arrived in Switzerland and elsewhere earlier and made the impression it did when it finally arrived, perhaps more people could have been saved."[42]

ON March 19, 1944, the day the Germans invaded Hungary, Vrba and Wetzler were still in Auschwitz, trying to memorize what they would tell the world if their escape succeeded. The Hungarian Jews, however, were not expecting the Germans to enter their country. On the eve of an Allied victory, those who had survived the first four and a half years of the war for the most part unharmed, were under the illusion that their long history of loyal service to the Magyar nation would continue to be recognized and that the Hungarian leaders would safeguard their basic interests. True, there were rumors about Auschwitz. Yet, with the Soviet army only 200 kilometers from the Hungarian border, the Jews felt they would be spared. They had no inkling that until the Third Reich finally collapsed, Hitler would relentlessly pursue his war against the Jews.[43]

March 19, 1944, was a sunny Sunday in Budapest, enabling Jews, like many others, to enjoy promenading along the banks of the Danube. Hanzi Brand, for example, the wife of the prominent Zionist activist Joel Brand, learned of the German invasion after she returned from a theater performance with her two children.[44]

March 19, 1944, was also a day that Eichmann would not forget easily. "I remember the date," he recalled before his trial in Jerusalem, "because it was my birthday. I crossed the border on March 19. And at 3:30 P.M. on Christmas Eve 1944, I left Budapest for the West."[45] He would further recall that he "went to Mauthausen concentration camp, because that's where they were holding the meeting in connection with the Hungarian program, which had to be kept secret, because the whole action, like all such things, was treated as top secret at Reich Security Headquarters."[46]

On March 19, Eichmann entered Hungary armed with detailed knowledge of Hungarian Jewry accompanied by two leading figures of the Sonderkommando, Hermann Alois Krumey and Dieter Wisliceny. He knew that he would not encounter any opposition: The community was confused, divided, compliant, with a non-resisting leadership, and easily subjected to isolation, expropriation, ghettoization, concentration, entrainment, and deportation.[47] With the limited manpower at his disposal, Eichmann essentially relied on five factors: (1) the secrecy of Auschwitz as the destination of the deportation, together with the effectiveness of the "resettlement" deception; (2) the cooperation of the anti-Semitic Hungarian forces; (3) a ready-made plan for deceiving the Jewish Council; (4) the hoary tradition of the Jews as obedient citizens; and (5) the divided and unprepared community and its leaders.[48]

Although there was little similarity with the situation in Warsaw, as the Hungarian Jewish community was widely scattered, its young men were in labor camps, and there was no underground organization, Eichmann took no chances. On April 3, he arrested Dr. Moshe Schweiger, one of the leaders of Zionist youth movement, who had managed to store 150 pistols, 40 grenades, 3 rifles, and 2 machine guns, and later sent him to Mauthausen.[49]

Eichmann was racing against time.

Some 800,000 Jews had to be liquidated, and who knew how much time was available, with German might shrinking on every front? . . . He brought with him to Budapest a top level team of assistants, all of whom had acquired wide experience as Eichmann's field directors in the countries of Europe and the Balkans—Herman Krumey, Wisliceny . . . Hunsche, Brunner . . . all experienced not only in the technical procedures of rounding up Jews and dispatching them to death camps. They were also familiar with all the arts of duplicity and deceit, allaying the suspicions of the Hungarians and the fears of the Jews by maintaining that the deportations were to "work camps" in the East. . . . To ensure that all went well at the receiving end, Eichmann called Rudolf Hoess, commandant of Auschwitz, to Budapest to co-ordinate arrangements. . . . Hoess thought Eichmann's program was too ambitious, and he was not sure that he could manage so many in so concentrated an operation. He wanted Eichmann to space deportations at wider intervals. The compromise they reached was for Eichmann to dispatch two trains one day and three the next. And this was done. In Auschwitz itself, the gas chambers and furnaces worked day and night. There were days when more people had been gassed than the crematorium could take, and bodies were burned in the open field. There were times when more than 10,000 Jews were killed in a single day.[50]

RELYING on Wisliceny's extensive experience in deporting 58,000 Jews from Slovakia (1942) and large numbers from Greece (1943), Eichmann could also bank on his deception skills. Wisliceny arrived in Hungary with a letter of recommendation from Weissmandel (in the name of the Slovak Working Group). According to Bauer, it was addressed to the "trustworthy" people with whom negotiations could be conducted in Hungary, "who were thought to have enough guts and devotion to negotiate with the SS as the Slovak group had done."[51] "Uncle Willy," Bauer further explains, was informed by the Slovak Working Group that these people were Rabbi von Freudiger, who represented the local Orthodox Jewish Council, Dr. Rezso Kasztner, an inspiration to the local Zionists, and Edith Weiss, the leader of the Reform Jewish group (who was in hiding).[52]

Wisliceny, Freudiger later reported,

closed the door and told me to sit down. Usually, we did not sit but remained standing. He told me: "I have a letter for you, read it." . . . I read the letter. It was a letter from Rabbi Weissmandel of blessed memory. It was written in Hebrew and was a short letter. He wrote to me that "finally fate has caught up with Hungarian Jewry" and suggested that I continue to deal with the Europe Plan that they had started with Wisliceny and that was known to me. In general, this was a letter expressing

confidence in Wisliceny, that we could negotiate with him. I read the letter. Wisliceny asked me: "Did you read it?" I answered: "Yes." "Did you
understand?" "Yes." "Return the letter to me," he said. I returned the
letter to him. He tore it into small pieces and threw it into the stove. After this he asked me: "What do you have to say to this letter?" I answered:
"I am at your disposal." He told me, "From now on, we need all the
money arriving from abroad." I asked him: "Do you mean 'we need' or
'I need'?" I wanted to know whether the deal was an official or a private
one. He told me: "This is none of your business." I had no reply to this.
Thereafter he told me: "You will hear from me again." That was all and
I left.[53]

We are not informed whether the deal with Wisliceny was indeed official or private. We do know that throughout May and June and early
July, the critical months of the deportations as well as of the dissemination of the Vrba-Wetzler report, Freudiger was one of the best informed members of the Jewish community.[54] He was privy not only to
the external dangers and eventually to the Vrba-Wetzler report but also
to the specifics: who was on the deportation lists. In his memoirs he
writes that when he found the name of his lawyer on the list he was
quick to counsel him "not to sleep at home that night.' Following this
advice, continues Freudiger, the lawyer "immediately contacted his
cousin who was a physician working in the largest mental hospital and
arranged for his immediate acceptance there. He remained there a few
weeks, and when he returned the lists were not timely any more."[55]

Acquaintance with the specific details of the Vrba-Wetzler Report
convinced Freudiger that his end was coming.

I received quite regularly mail from Bratislava, mainly from Rabbi
Weissmandel. . . . I found also a report of several pages of the statement
of two Jews who had miraculously succeeded in escaping from Auschwitz, and
now described with all the details what was going on in Auschwitz, the
particulars about the gas chambers, giving minute lists of when and how
many people were gassed—Jews, gypsies, etc., 1,750,000 in all—ending
that the gas chambers had now been put in good repair for the awaited

Hungarian Jews. Having read the protocol to its end I was shocked—I sat stunned for hours until at last my wife helped me up. The next morning, I took this protocol to the Council and showed it to a few of the members, who were all desperate. . . . We decided—unofficially—to spread the protocol and bring it to the knowledge of the more or less humane personalities of Hungarian society, politicians, etc.[56]

Seventeen years later Freudiger would testify at Eichmann's trial that he had received Weissmandel's warning letter "a few days before the fifteenth of May, on the tenth or eleventh."[57] He would later state that the Auschwitz protocols were translated into English by his assistants and that on June 19, 1944, they were sent out of Hungary through Krausz's special connections.[58] He would emphasize how relevant this information had been for him as prior to this date "*no one had any idea about Auschwitz.*"[59]

Thus informed, Freudiger reached the conclusion that "there was neither the time nor the possibility for organized resistance"[60] and therefore there was no point in informing the community but instead to arrange his own immediate escape. But this plan could be considered only on July 10, a day after Horthy stopped the deportations, when Freudiger approached Wisliceny at his lodging to find out what the plans for Budapest were.[61] On July 21, Wisliceny told him "in his casual way, '*Freudiger, you should go away now.*'"[62] On August 9, 1944, Freudiger and his eighty relatives boarded the train to freedom. Upon his arrival in Bucharest he engaged in documenting the chain of events that had led him to flee.[63] His memoirs include no note of regret regarding the panic that his escape created among the uninformed Jewish masses[64] who thought that his departure meant a resumption of the deportations. He would later immigrate to Israel where he soon came to be regarded as a distinguished educator.[65]

But those Hungarian Jews who were not informed about the report or its contents would not be so quick to forget.[66] In 1961, during Freudiger's testimony at Eichmann's trial, a Hungarian survivor screamed at him from the gallery, "You duped us so you could save yourselves and your families. But our families were killed." The man was apparently attacking Freudiger as a representative of the Jewish Council, for he added, referring to another Judenrat member, "He gave us injections to numb our minds. But he took his own parents out . . . and left mine there to die."[67] The court ordered the "uninformed" survivor to be silent and later had him removed from the gallery.

THREE

THE UNINFORMED

Of the three "trustworthy" individuals in Budapest whom the Slovak Working Group considered to have enough courage to negotiate with the Germans on behalf of the Hungarian community, only Dr. Rezsö Kasztner was left to follow their advice. Though the Zionist movement in Hungary comprised no more than five percent of all Hungarian Jews, Kasztner now desperately sought to use the movement imaginatively and to convince Eichmann that he had powerful connections with international Jewry, which would do all it could to please the Germans in order to rescue some Jews.[1] On April 5, two days before the escape of Vrba and Wetzler, and the day the Jews of Hungary began to wear the yellow star, Kasztner and Brand held their first meeting with the SS. They hoped to alleviate the anti-Jewish measures, and to initiate negotiations with the SS for the sake of saving six hundred holders of Palestine immigration certificates[2] in exchange for large sums of money. Wisliceny demanded two million dollars.

After the escape from Auschwitz, there was a sudden change in the speed of the negotiations, and the level of rank of those who took part in them. On April 21, the same day that Vrba and Wetzler made it back to their home-country Slovakia, Eichmann took charge of the bargaining.

The day of April 25, when Vrba and Wetzler were in the midst of dictating their report to Krasniansky, marked a dramatic turn in these "negotiations": Eichmann summoned the Zionist activist Joel Brand to his office in the Majestic Palace and proposed to him the grand scheme of "blood for trucks," a plan whose purpose numerous historians have not yet fully fathomed.[3] It sounded quite simple: "One million Jews for ten thousand trucks. One hundred Jews for each truck, a low price. But the trucks must be new, with all accessories, and they must be winterized. Throw in a few tons of coffee, tea, chocolate, and soap," Eichmann concluded.[4]

As a gesture to prove his goodwill, Eichmann also proposed a smaller plan, based on Himmler's consent to allow a train carrying the six hundred Hungarian Jews who had certificates for Palestine to leave Budapest for Switzerland. The man in charge would be Kurt Becher, Himmler's personal economic representative in Hungary, whom Himmler had told that he could promise the Jews anything, "but what we shall carry out is a different matter."[5] The bait was irresistible: Kasztner would be allowed to provide Eichmann with the list of passengers and he would be permitted to travel to his hometown Cluj to select the candidates for the train among his family friends and Zionist activists. The trip to Cluj was scheduled for May 4 and 5 with the Nazi's permission.[6]

Operatively, the grand plan would involve the dispatch of Joel Brand from Hungary on May 17, 1944, to have the Allies supply the Germans with the necessary commodities. Two days previously, massive daily deportations to Auschwitz of 12,000 Hungarian Jews had gone into full swing. The vacuum in leadership following Brand's departure was filled by Kasztner who, when he realized he could not persuade Eichmann to suspend the mass deportations, decided to resume the negotiations over the micro-plan aimed at averting deportation for at least a few.[7] He approached Eichmann in a number of meetings, during which he was made to stand for hours, at one point arrested briefly, and was even threatened with deportation to Auschwitz. At the end, Krumey's "consolation prize" of six hundred certificate holders, agreed upon on April 21, was confirmed by Eichmann on May 22. In the beginning of

May, when Kazstner was already in possession of the Vrba-Wetzler report, Kasztner was given permission to visit his hometown Cluj and allowed to add 388 people to the prospective train list. On June 10, when the Vrba-Wetzler report would finally reach the Hungarian Jewish leaders, the chosen passengers would be placed in a barracks specially built on Kolumbusz Street in Budapest and protected by five SS guards.[8]

The composition of the list was changed right up to the last moment, as Kasztner came under pressure from thousands of people, especially ultra-Orthodox and rich, assimilated Jews, asking to be included. No one expected the compilation of a just list, whether of 600, 1600, or more, of a community of 800,000 people.[9] Kasztner's final list consisted not only of the six hundred certificate holders and the selected Cluj people but also of Orthodox Jews (Freudiger's list), Neologue Jews (Stern's list), intellectuals and artists (Komoly's list), a selected group of Polish and Slovak refugees, selected members of Zionist movements, "paying passengers" whose contributions largely financed the transport, and relatives of the selecting committees—Weissmandel's father-in-law, Komoly's daughter, Kasztner's wife and daughter, Brand's sister, Stern's relative, and Biss's wife.[10] On June 30, the day of the scheduled departure, the transport officially consisted of approximately 1300 Jews. "However, during the delay caused by an air-raid, 450 Jews in the Bocskai Street synagogue climbed into the train under the cover of darkness (only 150 had been authorized to leave from there), as did a few dozen other Budapest Jews who heard about the special train."[11]

The train left Budapest at one o'clock in the night, between June 30 and July 1. It was escorted by SS and Hungarian soldiers. It would later carry many labels: the "test convoy" (Biss, 1973), the "prominent train" (Braham, 1981), the "rescue train" (Weitz, 1995), the "Bergen Belsen train" (Bauer, 1994), the "Kasztner train" (Cesarani, 1997), and "Kasztner's transport" (Braham, 2000).[12]

On June 20, ten days before the departure of the train, two full suitcases with the ransom were handed over to Kurt Becher by Hanzi Brand and her relative, Andreas Biss. The train's ransom was not to be the only Jewish money to find its way into Becher's pocket. In fact, it was small change compared with the biggest metal and machinery firm in Hungary, which he confiscated from the rich Jewish family of Manfred Weiss, or with what he received from his long-term plundering of the Warsaw ghetto by demanding a certain percentage of the goods taken from the Jews. But Becher's Nazi record is not restricted to economic issues. In the summer of 1941, Becher was already an operations officer in the first SS cavalry regiment in Russia, where his unit murdered at least 15,000 Jews.[13]

In April 1945, Becher produced as proof of his innocence the fact that he made his way to Mauthausen to return Kasztner's train money to Dr. Moshe Schweiger, who was close to death. Overwhelmed and uncertain whether he was hallucinating or not, Schweiger, who suddenly found himself a free person outside the camp with a suitcase filled with money, went trudging toward the Allied lines and handed this suitcase over to the first American unit he met; no one ever saw it again.[14] On August 4, 1947, Kasztner wrote an affidavit before Mr. Benno H. Selcke Jr., of the American evidence division of the international military tribunal in Nuremberg. In it he complimented Becher for being among "the very few SS leaders having the courage to oppose the program of annihilation of the Jews and to try to rescue human lives."[15] Dr. Moshe Schweiger would do the same on behalf of the Jewish Agency.[16]

Being locked in negotiations with the Germans is often cited as the reason that Kasztner was prevented from disseminating the Vrba-Wetzler report. But this seems not to be the only factor in his decision-making process. Kasztner believed that by persuading Eichmann "to make a 'goodwill gesture' and allow a trainload of Jews to be sent to a safe location pending the hoped-for wider agreement"[17] that he would set a precedent for more trains.[18] But this contrasts oddly with the position Kasztner set out in 1943 before eighty local Zionist youths: "We have to cope with a serious problem. We will not be able to save all the Hungarian Jews and the refugees who arrive daily from Poland, Slovakia, and Yugoslavia. The problem is whether we have the right to act like God, namely to decide who is to be saved and who is not. Do we morally have the right to save only part of the Jews? How will history come to judge us on the appointed day?"[19]

ONE might concur with the claim some historians have made that Kasztner was not the leader of the Hungarian Jews and so cannot be blamed for concealing information in general and the Vrba-Wetzler report in particular. But this claim carries little weight in respect to Kasztner's hometown. Cluj (or Kolozsvar in Hungarian) was the capital of Cluj County and of Hungarian-ruled northern Transylvania. It had about 100,000 citizens, 21,000 of them Jews, many of whom were highly educated. It boasted many politically active Zionist leaders. The internal affairs of the ghetto were entrusted to the Jewish Council. Kasztner's father-in-law, Dr. Joseph Fischer, was one of the richest people by the standards of those days. His family resided in a huge house, and he owned a car. He was president of the Cluj Jewish community and chairman of its Zionist society. Unlike in Budapest, many Jews in Cluj were of Zionist orientation, and the Zionist leaders carried significant moral influence. On May 4–5, 1944, when the ghettoization of the Cluj Jews started, Kasztner visited the town with Eichmann's permission. Although he was already in possession of the Vrba-Wetzler report, he did not share its contents with the local Jewish Council. Those 388 Cluj Jews who were marked for rescue in his train were placed in a camp on Kolumbusz Street in Budapest, where they were guarded by SS men.

In postwar accounts, some survivors from Cluj told how they peacefully boarded the train for Auschwitz, mistakenly believing themselves to be en route to a city named "Kenyermezo" in Hungarian (a fictitious name meaning bread field) for resettlement, entirely oblivious of the fact that they were heading for Auschwitz. Dr. Endre Balazs, the ghetto commander, who would later board the Kasztner train for Switzerland, had informed them that "the government of Hungary decided to evacuate the entire city of 'Kenyermezo,' in order to assemble in it all the Hungarian Jews until the end of the war. Just relax—you will live there with your entire family."[20]

Jacob Freifeld and his family went on one of the early trains for

Kenyermezo. "After the first train left Cluj," he later testified, "all the Jews were assembled in the ghetto. Kohani [one of Kasztner's group] jumped up on a platform and read aloud a letter he said was from a Jewish family in Kenyermezo. The letter said that whole family was working at good jobs and were all in good health and being well taken care of. I had a friend, Hillel Danzig (an activist who played a prominent role in the Zionist movement in Cluj and later became a leading Israeli journalist). We worked together earlier in the Ukraine camps. In Cluj I asked him, 'What's the truth about those letters Kohani read in public? Are they really true?' He told me, 'Yes, they are true.' And he gave me a tip I should try to go to Kenyermezo as soon as I could, because the first arrivals there would get the best places."[21] Freifeld's family was incinerated in Auschwitz. Hillel Danzig did not board this train. He went on Kasztner's train to Switzerland. He later reluctantly admitted that he knew he was being taken to a safe place, and he knew also that Freifeld would be taken to a place much worse.[22] In his postwar testimony Kasztner did not hide the grim fact that *"it was the task of the Judenrat to decide who would go first, who later."*[23]

The 1990 Israeli *Encyclopedia of the Holocaust* summarizes the morality of the Cluj deportation briefly using the passive voice: "Kasztner, who had been in the midst of controversial negotiations with Eichmann's Sonderkommando on a rescue arrangement, visited the city on May 4 and 5. Shortly thereafter, 388 Jews, including many of Kasztner's relatives and closest friends, *were taken* out of the ghetto and transferred to Budapest. From there, together with some 1,300 other Jews, they *were eventually taken* to Switzerland via Bergen Belsen—a rescue mission that engendered great controversy."[24] Information about some aspects of this controversy is found in Braham: "Instead of going with the masses to Kenyermezo to provide continued leadership, most of them [the Judenrat leaders] eagerly joined the Kasztner group that was taken to Budapest—with the aid of the SS."[25]

In this context, the claim that the Vrba-Wetzler report had received widespread, albeit unofficial, publicity within Jewish Hungary seems quite problematic.[26] On June 10, 1944, Dr. Imre Varga, a young Budapest physician, questioned the Jewish Council on why they did not organize resistance, halt the "cowardly submission," and adopt more suitable methods to prevent total catastrophe.[27] Samu Stern, the head of the Hungarian Jewish Council answered that "the Jewish Council is doing everything in its power" to prevent the deportations.[28] Although it was already one-and-a-half months since the secret of Auschwitz had been revealed, the details of the killings provided by the Vrba-Wetzler report were still generally unknown.[29] Samu Stern could say only that Jews were being taken in freight cars "to unknown places, to extermination."[30] In his postwar memoirs he further stated that he knew what they had done in all German-occupied states of Europe but failed to mention the Vrba-Wetzler report.[31]

One may well argue (though there is no evidence for it) that on June 10, two groups of Jews were probably given two different types of information: Dr. Varga and his people in Budapest were given *general* information about the extermination, but on the same day 388 selected prominent Jews from Cluj were given *specific* information about Auschwitz. When their train stopped at Auschpitz, a town in the Czech Moravian Protectorate, the passengers were panic-stricken and when it arrived at Linz in Austria they refused to take showers.[32] That they reacted that way runs counter to what we know of the secrecy and the selective use of the report.

Kasztner's activity in the selective rescue lasted until the end of the war. According to Bauer, on March 31, 1945 (three days before Russian troops liberated Bratislava), Kasztner was able to rescue Rabbi Michael Dov Weissmandel and twenty-seven other people from a hiding place in Slovakia (together with twenty-two more from Vienna) and take them to Switzerland.[33] The purpose of this rescue mission at that time and place remains unclear, and the writings about it even more so. "Rabbi Michael Dov Weissmandel [deported in autumn of 1944] managed while still in Slovakian territory to leap from the Auschwitz-bound train. He joined a group of underground refugees in Bratislava and in February, 1945, *was moved* with the rest of the group to a hideout in Switzerland with Rudolf Kasztner's assistance."[34]

This strange rescue effort from Bratislava on the eve of the city's liberation by the Russians was conducted with the help of Hermann

Krumey, an Obersturmbanhfuhrer in the Waffen-SS, an active member of the security police in Lodz, and later a leading member in Eichmann's Sonderkommando in Hungary. Regardless of Krumey's efficiency in arranging at least six transports from the Zamosc area to Auschwitz, Kasztner credited him for this "helping" activity at the end of the war. Kasztner signed an affidavit on Herman Krumey's behalf on May 5, 1948, that resulted in the latter's release from Allied custody, where he had been held since May 1945. Krumey was again arrested in 1960. After a trial in Frankfurt in 1965, at which Vrba testified as a witness, he was first condemned to five years hard labor and later, on August 29, 1969 (when Vrba again was a witness), to life imprisonment. The conviction was upheld by the federal court in Germany on January 17, 1973.[35]

A small calculation suggests that, if only one percent of the 437,000 Hungarian Jewish victims had been persuaded of the truth of the report and had chosen not to board the boxcar trains to Auschwitz, almost three times 1,684 Jews could probably have been saved. That the opportunity to read the report opened the eyes of some is shown by the case of Professor George Klein, later to become a member of the Nobel Prize committee in Stockholm. As a youngster at that time, Klein worked in the service of the Jewish Council in Budapest. He writes:

I was shown [the Vrba-Wetzler report] by one of the members of the Jewish Council in Budapest in *greatest secrecy,* only a few weeks after it had been written. I still remember the mixture of nausea and intellectual satisfaction I felt when I first read what later became known as "the Auschwitz Report." Nausea, because I realized that I was reading about the fate of my beloved grandmother, my uncles, and many other relatives and friends who had already been deported from my father's village in the Northeast. I also knew that I was reading *about my own most probable fate.* The paradoxical but very distinct intellectual satisfaction stemmed from the fact that this was the first text that made sense. Nothing else that we were told or were telling each other made any sense whatsoever. The dry, nearly scientific language of the report, the naked facts and the seemingly passionless objectivity of the report made a stronger impact than a thousand emotional outbursts. It was this report that prompted me to escape. Only the definite knowledge of what was waiting at the other end of the railway line overcame my fear of being caught and shot.[36]

As a delivery boy of the Judenrat in Budapest, George Klein had seen Kasztner at work during this critical period of time and admired him:

> I was working there, first as an errand boy and later as secretary to one of the members of the council. I knew that Kasztner was trying to select a number of people for rescue, but that I had no chance of being included in that privileged group. Nevertheless, he was a hero in my eyes, and he remained so in the years that followed. He rescued many while the rest of us tried to save only ourselves or, at best, the members of our families.[37]

Indeed, Kasztner hoped to recruit the Germans for further rescue missions, assuming that small numbers of Jews would make no difference in their large-scale murder plans. This logic is echoed in Eichmann's explanation to the correspondent of *Life* magazine on November 28 and December 5, 1960:

> In Hungary my basic orders were to ship all the Jews out of Hungary in as short a time as possible. Now after years of working behind a desk, I had come out into the raw reality of the field. . . . they had sent me, the "master" himself, to make sure the Jews did not revolt as they had in the Warsaw Ghetto. . . . In obedience to Himmler's directive I now concentrated on negotiations with the Jewish political officials in Budapest. . . . Among them [was] Dr. Rudolph Kasztner, authorized representative of the Zionist movement. This Dr. Kasztner was a young man about my age, an ice-cold lawyer and a fanatical Zionist. He agreed to help keep the Jews from resisting deportation—and even keep order in the collection camps—if I would close my eyes and let a few hundred or a few thousand young Jews emigrate illegally to Palestine. It was a good bar-

gain. For keeping order in the camps, the price . . . was not too high for me. . . . We trusted each other perfectly. . . . with his great polish and reserve he would have made an ideal Gestapo officer himself.

——————

AFTER the war some "uninformed" Jews appeared to agree with Eichmann's assessment of Kasztner's personality and moral philosophy. In January 1954, an unknown Israeli citizen, Malkiel Greenwald, who had lost fifty-two family members in the Auschwitz concentration camp, accused Dr. Kasztner, who had become a well-known political activist, of collaboration with the Nazis. Kasztner, who stood for the Knesset on behalf of Mapai (the ruling Labor party), brought a libel suit against this non-Mapai accuser. Shmuel Tamir, a brilliant young non-Mapai lawyer who defended Greenwald, succeeded in steering the trial into a thorough examination of the role played by the war-time Jewish leaders in the efforts to rescue the Hungarian Jews. This may help explain why Greenwald, the defendant, became the de facto accuser and the court had to decide whether one or all of the four allegations against Kasztner—that he (1) had been a collaborator with the Nazis, (2) had helped the Nazis to pave the way to the murder of the Hungarian Jews, (3) had benefited from the Nazi theft, and (4) had saved Nazis after the war—had any merit. Thus, it could happen that the Greenwald trial, transformed into a political trial through the use of language and literary metaphors, became the Kasztner trial.[38]

In effect, although he himself was not a member of the official Hungarian Judenrat, Kasztner's trial became a trial against the Judenrat. It is not exactly clear how this happened as there were, of course, other ex-members of Judenrate in the new State of Israel. One cannot exclude the fact that many of the surviving Jewish leaders retained their positions of power by staying close to the country's establishment and its main political parties. Some of them soon would occupy important positions in the nascent state. As Zertal explains, the law, of course, did not have these people in mind.[39]

On June 22, 1955, the Jerusalem District Court, presided over by Judge Benjamin Halevi, accepted most of Tamir's arguments, among them an affidavit given by Kasztner on behalf of Kurt Becher. Halevi even went so far as to quote Virgil "Timeo Danaos et dona ferentes" [Beware of Greeks bearing gifts] and ruled that in accepting the gift of the "freedom train," Kasztner had "sold his soul to the devil." This "sale" had three aspects: First, his negotiations with the Nazis for the sake of rescuing his Cluj family, his friends, and a select group of Zionists and the rich; second, his collaboration with the Nazis' ploy to silence the Hungarian Jews; and third, the voluntary help he rendered to Nazi criminals to escape justice after the war.

Halevi decided to focus his judgment on the contract allegedly signed between Eichmann and Kasztner. According to Bilsky, Halevi, following the spirit of contract law, saw the "negotiations" as done between two equal parties and tended to ignore the historical time in which Kasztner's action had taken place. "This approach," concluded Bilsky, "facilitated the attribution of absolute responsibility to Kasztner for the consequences of his actions—the deaths of approximately 400,000 Hungarian Jews."[40] Kasztner argued that "he had not intended . . . to replace the main contract to rescue the whole Hungarian Jewry but to test the Nazi's intentions."[41]

With massive legal help from Mapai, Kasztner appealed to the Supreme Court. On March 4, 1957, he was shot by a young extremist near his Tel Aviv home. He died ten days later. None of Kasztner's train passengers published an obituary.[42] Kasztner did not live to learn that the five Supreme Court judges who heard the appeal overturned the lower court's ruling in a split decision. All five upheld Judges Halevi's verdict on the "criminal and perjurous manner" in which Kasztner after the war had "without justification" saved several Nazi war criminals. Judge Silberg, whose parents had vanished in the Holocaust, upheld Judge Halevi's finding that Kasztner had collaborated with the Nazis during the war.

The majority opinion, written by Judge Shimon Agranat and read on January 15–17, 1958, cleared Kasztner of the stigma of "collaboration," rejecting the metaphoric conclusion of Judge Halevi, that Kasztner had "sold his soul to the Devil." Justice Agranat favored a contextual/historical approach to Kasztner's case rather than an abstract/scientific one—he saw him as a hero who had his limits in a given chaotic historical time, and the event itself as a narrative that entails no closure. Agranat argued that the moral and historical judgments they were being forced to make should never have reached the courtroom and that "the proper form, if there was one, was a public commission for historians."[43] He concluded that Kasztner's sole motivation had been the rescue of all Hungarian Jews and that his behavior on the date of his visit to Cluj (May 4–5) and thereafter both actively (the "Kasztner train" plan for prominent Jews) and passively (not conveying the "Auschwitz news" and not encouraging large-scale resistance) accorded with his devotion to his role as organizer of the rescue in Budapest. Supreme Court Judge Moshe Silberg insisted on unfolding the puzzle: How did the fully informed Kasztner behave in the face of the uninformed Cluj Jewish community? Was Kasztner the one who had decided not to disclose to the local leaders the secrets of Auschwitz? Or were the informed leaders the ones who blocked this message? Was there a third possibility?

The Israeli Labor Party leaders would never forgive Halevi for his 1955 judgment. A few years later, the Israeli government did not want him to sit on the 1961 Eichmann trial. It feared that Halevi might probe too deeply into the behavior of Jewish leaders during the Holocaust.[44]

One may wonder if the five Supreme Court judges would have reasoned the same way had they known that Kasztner gave postwar affidavits not only on behalf of Kurt Becher and Herman Krumey (Eichmann's deputy) but also, as was discovered only later, on behalf of SS-Obergruppenfuhrer Hans Juttner, chief of the SS-Fuhrungshauptamt (SS Operational Main Office). In 1947, Kasztner tried in vain to save Wisliceny by handing him over to the British for "further investigation"—Wisliceny would be executed by the Slovaks.[45] As Robert Kempner, a senior official at the Nuremberg trial, remarked, Kasztner was running around at Nuremberg looking for Nazis he could save.[46]

Over the years some Israeli historians have made numerous attempts to provide alternative explanations for the motives that could have prompted Kasztner to testify on behalf of these war criminals.[47]

For example:

1. "Kasztner made his recommendation [on behalf of Becher] at a time when he knew . . . that Becher had extorted money from Jews, *though he could not have known the background of his Nazi protector.*"
2. "We must put things in perspective: *Kasztner helped others besides Becher;* he was willing to certify the humanity of SS General Hans Juttner, he was willing to help Wisliceny, and he wrote letters whitewashing Krumey (February 5, 1947) and Kettliz (October 13, 1947)."
3. "From a perusal of these letters and testimonies about Kasztner, the picture emerges of an ambitious and courageous man *who wanted to tell the truth about people who had helped him.*"
4. Becher "acted in those days like a convicted Nazi who saw the Third Reich crumbling around him and was trying *to maintain his own position by saving lives.*[48]

The 1990 Israeli *Encyclopedia of the Holocaust* presents the event in the following way: "Kasztner's line seems to have been one of *noblesse oblige:* once the war was over, any Nazi who had made a gesture or taken action in favor of Jews should be recognized for it."[49] Many documents have yet to be published, among them a tape recording from Eichmann's trial that discussed the question of Becher's collaboration with the Jews but was censored upon the instruction of a "higher authority."[50]

In early 1996, more than fifty years after the escape of Vrba and Wetzler from Auschwitz, Israel TV would still not be able to mention any of the names of the five and only successful Jewish escapees. No documentary has ever been made about them. But it did allocate prime time to an interview with the now multimillionaire Kurt Becher.

PART TWO

BETWEEN AUSCHWITZ AND JERUSALEM: VRBA SILENCED

All vanishes except the memory.

ALBERT CAMUS

Renowned Holocaust historians in North America and Europe provide clear and unambiguous information about the escapees and their names, while the role of the Vrba-Wetzler report is generally given adequate mention in most histories of the Holocaust.[1] In his book on Admiral Horthy, Professor Thomas Sakmyster claims that Horthy's decision to prevent the deportation of the Budapest Jews was a direct result of his reading of the Vrba-Wetzler Report; up to that point he had dismissed information about Auschwitz as gossip or "Jewish exaggeration."[2] The Vrba-Wetzler report plays an important role in the renewed discussion of why Auschwitz wasn't bombed. This question, write the authors of *The Bombing of Auschwitz*, "is one of the most basic questions that students of the Holocaust ask. It ranks alongside 'Why didn't the Jews resist?'"[3]

The representation of the escape from Auschwitz in history textbooks in the Hebrew language takes two main forms: First, a technical one, such as limited references to anonymous escapees or no reference at all.[4] Second, a conceptual form (that is, one of marginalization), whereby the escapees and their actions are mentioned but their contri-

53

bution is regarded as minimal.[5] How should we understand the above phenomenon of "historical autism," as Bedurftig defines it?[6]

According to B.C. McCullagh, there are four ways in which historical narrative might be biased.

> First, historians sometimes misinterpret evidence, so that they are not justified in asserting that the inferences they draw about what happened in the past are true. . . . Second, when historians compile an account of a historical subject so that it is unbalanced or what I call *unfair* [emphasis in the original]. . . . The third kind of bias is that of a general description of the past that implies facts which, on the evidence available, are known to be false. . . . A fourth common form of bias in history occurs in providing causal explanations of historical events when some, but not all, of the important causes are mentioned, so that the reader gets a misleading impression of the process by which the event came about.

McCullagh further suggests that most often biases in historical inference, description, interpretation, and explanation "can all occur accidentally, by mistakes, through an oversight. In that case we would not call them biased but just wrong or unjustified. They are only *biased* if they occur because the historian wants the outcome she has produced, normally to further certain interests that she has."[7]

An interesting example of a biased history is found in the writings of Albright's father, Joseph Korbel whose parents and wife's mother had perished in the Holocaust, some in the family camp.

In 1948 the Korbel family was granted political asylum in the United States after the Communist coup in Czechoslovakia, and Joseph Korbel became a professor of international relations at the University of Colorado. He eventually became dean of the Graduate School of International Studies there. During that time he wrote five scholarly books about modern Eastern European history, in which he barely mentioned the fate of the Jews in World War II, the most horrific chapter in the entire period of his expertise. In his 1977 book *Twentieth-Century Czechoslovakia: The Meaning of Its History,* published almost thirty years after he arrived in America, Korbel notes the existence of concentration camps almost as an aside and makes fewer than a dozen minor references to the Czechoslovak Jewish population that was virtually wiped out by Hitler. Dobbs argues that unlike the state-imposed historical bias, Korbel's historical amnesia was a personal choice, typical of some first-generation Americans who want to forget the past and start a new life.[8] Others believed that "Korbel had an uncanny instinct for survival, an instinct that caused him to surrender his name, his citizenship, and his politics and to bury his religious heritage. Korbel seemed to want to forget not only his roots but even the Holocaust itself."[9]

One may argue that some forms of bias in history parallel family secrets with some information remaining inaccessible or invisible to others. Family secrets involve managing information in a manner that creates identities, advantages, and disadvantages of knowing, by keeping certain bits of knowledge hidden to avoid observability by others. One common method of secret keeping is the *information void*, which involves purposely withholding facts from others. This strategy is used only when individuals outside the secret do not anticipate that there is information to be received. *Falsification or commission* is used instead when information is anticipated, so that those who receive it are unable to judge its accuracy. Consequently, the unaware persons are forced to acquire or retain a false belief or to cease to believe the truth. Another common method families use to conceal their secrets is *clouding*, namely presenting details in a manner that misleads the inquirers into believing that the correct information has been made available. Here the secrets are maintained by not correcting a falsehood.[10]

In what follows, I make an effort to trace the use the family of Israeli historians have made of misnaming, misreporting, miscrediting and misrepresenting in the secretive tale of the escape from Auschwitz.

We are frequently told that German historiography is dominated by a tendency "to hide things, not to explicate them."[11] Are Germans the only historians not immune to the banality of official historiography?

FOUR

MISNAMING

The arrival of the escapees in Slovakia was a dramatic moment for the Working Group and an unexpected historical bonus. The encounter took place around naming. Upon their arrival, the escapees' names were verified against the deportation list. Upon their departure, their original names were replaced by false ones. How then did it happen that one of the commonest forms of omission became the failure of the wartime Jewish leaders, as well as some Holocaust historians, to recall the names of the escapees? One of the first to make an anonymous documented reference to the escapees was Dr. Oskar Neumann. In his 1956 memoir, he writes the following:

> News about the horror of Auschwitz had reached Slovakia before, but it was vague. . . . Who is it who can reach death and come back? But one day this miracle happened. On that day, *two young Jewish chaps*, Slovakian-born, who had been deported in 1942 to Auschwitz, appeared. Their identity could be verified from their housing report (above the serial number tattooed on their arms). As in a thriller, they had managed to escape . . . and by an impossible route reached the Slovakian border, at the small town of Cadca.

"*These chaps*," he further related, "did also report that recently an enormous construction project had been initiated in the camp and very recently the SS often spoke about looking forward to the arrival of '*Hungarian salami*.'"[1]

Anonymity, for the protection of the informants as well as of those who recorded them, was originally maintained also by Neumann's assistant, Oskar Krasniansky, who spent three intensive days interrogating the escapees and six hours in an important "conference meeting" with the Vatican legate.[2] But in his depositions for the Eichmann trial, which are replete with the exact names and precise details of others, Krasniansky seems to have simply failed to recall the escapees' names. He testified that the report was written "by myself" in the spring of 1944, from the words of "*two young people* who succeeded in escaping from the death camps of Auschwitz (Birkenau) in April, 1944."[3]

Livia Rothkirchen,[4] whom most historians regard as a prominent expert on the Slovak community,[5] quotes Wetzler's testimony in her 1961 book and refers to Vrba by name. In her 1974 writings, Rothkirchen refers to the Auschwitz escapees as "*two young men*" who were the first prisoners to succeed in escaping from the camp.[6] Bauer's early writings followed this line of omission as well. In 1978 he wrote: "Detailed reports regarding the Auschwitz death camp and the gassing installations in it were received in Slovakia from *two Slovak Jews* who escaped from the camp on 7 April 1944."[7] Rothkirchen furthermore downplays the fact that the Vrba-Wetzler report or its content was the first report from Auschwitz that reached Switzerland. She does not clarify for the reader that the initial information sent to the Hungarian leaders, as well as to the West, at the end of April or in early May, must have been based solely on the Vrba-Wetzler report, because the information provided by the Rosin and Mordowicz report became available only in the middle of June.[8]

This form of clouding is perpetuated further by the younger generation of researchers. Dina Porat, a specialist in the attitude of the Yishuv to the Holocaust, wrote in 1990:

> It was not known what Auschwitz was or what was the role of Birkenau, the killing place within Auschwitz that devoured the arrivals there, who were never to return. Today, in retrospect, it is hard to understand how it could not have been known, but the letters and the documents speak for themselves. The way the Germans succeeded in concealing the role

and central position of Auschwitz, and preventing information leaking out of it until June 1944, is still surprising today. It is hard for people who held various positions in Israel or in the Jewish leadership in the free world to believe that in fact only after April 1944—when *two young Slovak Jews* escaped from Auschwitz and brought a detailed report and exact drawings to Bratislava—only then did the Western world learn what this place was.[9]

In the English version of her book, Porat writes:

In April 1944 *two Jewish prisoners* escaped from Auschwitz to Slovakia and were the first to reach a place where Jewish organizations and Jewish leadership still operated and could convey their message further. Both had worked for two years in the registration office of the camp and thus could supply information about the structure of the camp, the names of its commanders, its procedures, and especially the course of the extermination. Their testimony reached Geneva along with additional information from two more Jewish prisoners who had escaped from Auschwitz at the end of May, after the annihilation of Hungarian Jewry had already begun[10]

Porat cites Gilbert's *Auschwitz and the Allies* as her source.[11] Gilbert provides the full names of the escapees. Porat does not explain why she decided to omit them.

An interesting historical position is that taken by the late Israeli historian Asher Cohen, a Hungarian child survivor of the Holocaust. In his writings in Hebrew with Kohn, Cohen summarized the events as follows: "On May 24 *two young people* who escaped from Auschwitz arrived in Slovakia, and they brought the first and most detailed information about the structure and functioning of the death camp. This report is known in Holocaust literature as the Auschwitz Protocol."[12] In 1994, Cohen met Vrba at a conference held in Washington, D.C., on the fiftieth anniversary of the Holocaust in Hungary. But in an article published two years later, the names of the escapees were still missing.

The "Auschwitz Protocols" is a detailed report on the camp and the process of extermination that went on there, which was delivered by *two young Slovaks* who managed to escape from Auschwitz. Their report did reach Hungary and was available to the leaders of the Jewish Council, the heads of the Zionist movement, church leaders, and many political leaders in Hungary in early May 1944.[13]

In the 1990 edition of the Israeli *Encyclopedia of the Holocaust,* the escapees are mentioned in the entry on Auschwitz as follows:

A well-known successful escape was that of two young Jews, Alfred Wetzler and Walter Rosenberg (Rudolf Vrba), on April 7, 1944. The two managed to reach Bratislava and contact some of the Jewish leaders still remaining there. They wrote a very detailed report on Auschwitz that was smuggled out to the free world (see Auschwitz protocols[14]).

This form of acknowledgment disappears in the 2001 edition of the *Holocaust Encyclopedia,* compiled by Walter Lacqueur and Judith Taylor Baumel. Rinat-ya Gorodznik, who is affiliated with the Institute of Contemporary Jewry at the Hebrew University of Jerusalem, writes in its "Chronology of Holocaust": "7 April 1944: Auschwitz Protocols: *two Jewish prisoners* escape from Auschwitz and pass to the papal representatives in Slovakia a detailed report on the killings in the camp."[15]

In 1944, the rationale adduced for suppressing the escapees' names was that it was for their own protection. This explanation for non-naming, conceived at the time the report was written and maintained for several decades by Israeli historians, is problematic and more than embarrassing: If the Gestapo knew the names and their warrants were set out neatly and legibly so that any ordinary policeman in Germany and its satellite states could understand them, who else was there to fear?[16]

FIVE

MISREPORTING

Ironically, among those who benefited the most from the misnaming that surrounded Vrba and Wetzler were Holocaust deniers. While various neo-Nazi authors make extraordinary efforts to delegitimize Vrba's testimony in his report and his memoirs, the belated acknowledgment that comes from some Israeli Holocaust historians only serves to discredit Vrba and Wetzler even further.

The first Holocaust denier to observe the *information void* and *omission* of the escape from Auschwitz in Israeli Holocaust historiography was Arthur Butz.[1] A professor of electrical engineering at Northwestern University, Butz is the author of *The Hoax of the Twentieth Century*. This "landmark" work in denial literature argues that the entire story of the Holocaust was invented by the Jews to further their Zionist ends. While Butz's work cannot be taken as serious historical research— rather the reverse—it was nevertheless seen as a provocation in historical circles because it hit a nerve.

Butz examined the postwar memoirs of Oskar Neumann's 1956 *Im Schatten des Todes*[2] and noticed two crucial facts: First, Dr. Neumann does not mention the names of the escapees. Second, he does not mention the Vrba-Wetzler report, although, as Butz knows, the recording of the escapees' account was undertaken in the most meticulous and professional manner under his aegis as a skillful lawyer. As a result of this reading, Butz developed a theory that if the content of the Vrba-Wetzler report were true, Israeli historians would certainly know the escapees' names and would have publicized their report. Butz concluded:

61

"Neumann had been one of the leaders of the various Jewish Councils and resistance organizations in Slovakia. . . . In Neumann's story the two young Slovak Jews appear on schedule in Slovakia. . . . Neumann gives the impression that he actually met these people. . . . His account does not."[3] Indeed, one can see that Neumann writes in a emotional form about the escapees—he is well informed about them but does not report the most relevant details.

Butz further reminds Israeli Holocaust historians that "Vrba's affidavit at the Eichmann trial was rejected by the court on the grounds that there was no excuse for the prosecution not bringing him to testify" in person.[4] To support the alleged fabrication of Vrba's story, Butz quotes Erich Kulka's article in which he discredits Rudolf Vrba for calling himself Rudi in his memoirs in reference to a time when he was still named Walter Rosenberg.[5] Indeed, in the course of his criticism, Kulka does not remind his readers that Vrba's memoirs had been written after the war, when Walter Rosenberg had legalized his nom de guerre of Rudolf Vrba. Butz quotes Kulka: "In the book the other prisoners refer to him as Rudi" and also criticize him for revealing the names of Rosin and Mordowicz.[6] He writes, "I know nothing of these people [Rosin and Mordowicz] other than that they remained quiet about their heroic exploits for an even greater number of years than Vrba and Wetzler did." Butz further claims that the report itself was a fabrication, probably invented by the pro-Zionists in Washington attached to the War Refugee Board. When Professor Conway confronted this thesis by comparing the text of the report sent to the Vatican in June 1944 with that received in Washington, they were found to be identical, showing Butz's claim that the whole thing was invented in America to be baseless.[7]

Another Holocaust denier who follows this questioning is Robert Faurisson. He asserts that the gas chambers did not exist and that the burden is on the historians to prove that they did. This former professor of literature at the University of Lyons II is puzzled as well when he comes to explain the Auschwitz "myth."

We have known for some time that the Auschwitz myth is of an exclusive Jewish origin. . . . The principal authors of the creation and the peddling of the "rumor of Auschwitz" have been, successively, *two Slovaks, Alfred Wetzler (or Weczler) and Rudolf Vrba (or Rosenberg or Rosenthal)*. . . . It is remarkable that from beginning to end that story comes from essentially or perhaps even exclusively Jewish sources. Two Jewish liars (Vrba and Wetzler) from Slovakia convinced or seem to have convinced other Jews from Hungary, Switzerland, the United States, Great Britain and Poland. This is not a conspiracy or a plot; it is the story of the birth of a religious belief: the Myth of Auschwitz.[8]

In the 1990s, possibly embarrassed by the taunts of Holocaust deniers casting doubt on the existence of the gas chambers, some Israeli Holocaust historians suddenly resurrected the escapees' names. Thus, exactly fifty years after their escape, the jejune vocabulary of "two Slovak Jews" and "two chaps" was at last replaced by a living body possessed of a name, who was now treated as a "hero."[9]

The re-emergence of Vrba's name in the 1990s in some of the English and Hebrew writings of leading Israeli historians is no less interesting than its absence in publications prior to this period.[10] Is it because some historians have attained seniority and "are now nearing retirement [and] their work has reached maturation"?[11] The data suggest that even now the policy of "Holocaust cosmetics" was partial: Rudolf Vrba is called either Rosenberg-Vrba, Vrba-Rosenberg or Rosenberg W.[12]

The uninformed reader is not referred to the escapees' memoirs, even when their names are cited in the correct form and consequently must rely on the labeling of the text.[13] This form of commission was again seized on by Holocaust deniers in 2000. David Irving, who contended that "none died in Auschwitz's notorious gas chambers," was fully aware of the names Vrba and Wetzler, whom Professor Deborah E. Lipstadt, the scholar who sued in this libel trial, described as "young Jews."[14]

Leading scholars at the United States Holocaust Museum, who keep close ties with Yad Vashem, seem to follow this form of omission with commission. One can find in small letters the name "Rudolf Vrba, an escapee from Auschwitz," as a signature for a quotation in which he describes the Auschwitz ramp.[15] Why was the caption about the incoming trains the only avenue through which Vrba's moral knowledge was deemed worthy of affecting museum visitors?

The Hebrew inscription outlining the Auschwitz escape that appears on a wall of the Yad Vashem Museum in Jerusalem attests that it was accomplished by "two young Slovak Jews." In a phone conversation with the former director of the Israeli Holocaust Museum in Yad Vashem (March 1998), I was informed that the wording "two Slovak Jews" was in keeping with Museum policy, "as no names are mentioned." But the following day when I joined a students' tour led by a museum guide, I could clearly observe how her method of explanation differed at two sites. She briefly touched on the escape of two anonymous young Slovaks from Auschwitz. However, at the picture of inmates in the barracks in Buchenwald she stopped and asked the students if they could name one of them. When they could not, she pointed out, "This is Eli Wiesel."[16]

SIX

MISCREDITING

Vrba and Wetzler did not leave the telling of their story to the historians. They themselves documented the narrative of their escape, Wetzler writing in the Eastern bloc and Vrba in the West. Wetzler's first account, under the pseudonym Joseph Lanik,[1] was titled *Auschwitz, Tomb of Four Million People.* It was written in Slovak and summarizes the Vrba-Wetzler–Rosin-Mordowicz report. In 1964 he published a second book in Slovak, a fictionalized account under the same pen name, called *What Dante Did Not See.*[2] Vrba's book was published in English, in London in 1963 and in New York in 1964.[3] It can be argued that Wetzler's books, because they were published during the Cold War under the rules of Communist censorship then in force in Czechoslovakia, were hard to come by. But Vrba's book was published in numerous Western European languages, including English, which is the language most widely read in the Israeli academy. It can hardly be claimed, therefore, that it was not known to Israeli Holocaust historians. Attention could further have been aroused by the many reviews it elicited in leading papers around the world as well as in numerous Jewish periodicals in Britain, the United States, Germany, France, Holland, and Canada. Yet, although most Israeli historians admit that Vrba and Wetzler were "the most informative of the escapees,"[4] the reader is referred to Neumann's memoirs,[5] which they regard as "highly reliable when contrasted with the documentation."[6]

This reference is problematic if we define credibility as the weight given to a particular testimony.[7] After all, how can one rank Dr. Neumann's memoirs as highly credible if he failed to include the warning to the Hungarian Jews in the Vrba-Wetzler report that he was so careful in preparing?

In her doctoral thesis (supervised by Bauer), entitled *"The Jewish Center UZ: An Organization of Collaborators or a Rescue Group?,"*[8] Dr. Gila Fatran treats Dr. Neumann's memoirs as apologetic and portrays his decision making as often not realistic and even destructive. In her 1992 book, which was based on her dissertation, Fatran omits the word collaborators,[9] while her new title is a neutral one: *The Leadership of Slovakian Jews in the Holocaust 1938–1944.* Here, Fatran no longer discusses the fact that the final version of the Vrba-Wetzler report, composed under Neumann's aegis, omitted the warning to the Hungarian Jews,[10] nor does she include Neumann's failure to recall this event in his memoirs. She does cite them as one of the most credible sources of information for most of the historians of the Slovak community. As Dominick La Capra[11] observed, it is still a puzzle "how texts classified as great or as classic are construed . . . repressed or downplayed in canonical interpretations—processes that may in certain situations have broader social and political consequences."[12]

In Bauer's best-known Hebrew textbook, *The Holocaust: Some Historical Aspects,* the young Israeli reader is informed about the escape from Auschwitz in one sentence: "Detailed reports about the death camp in Auschwitz and the gas chambers there were received in Slovakia from *two Slovak Jews who escaped from Auschwitz* on April 7. Two additional testimonies were received from two other fugitives who escaped on May 27." The reader is not told how or whether these data helped to save Jews. Instead, credit is given to Weissmandel, Kasztner, and Mayer, who are described as "persistent and heroic individuals" who "understood the severity of the situation and eventually saved Jews."[13]

It is not until 1997 that Vrba appears in Bauer's writings as a most reliable eyewitness.[14] This occurred when he was given an opportunity by the prestigious German journal *Vierteljahrshefte für Zeitgeschichte* to respond to the testimony in an article Vrba had published the previous year and which the journal accepted as credible.[15] But even this belated praise was not without clouding. Bauer reminds his readers that the data on the expansion of the gas chambers in Auschwitz are missing in the Vrba-Wetzler report.[16] Bauer sees no need to explain to his readers that the report contained a description of the new railway construction. Nor does he mention that it had been Dr. Neumann's decision whether or not to include the alarming message regarding the Hungarian Jews in the report. This mode of writing makes room for the reader to suspect that the prediction of the liquidation of the Hungarian Jews was a post-war invention of the escapees, as some researchers chose to mention.[17] In line with Certeau, one wonders what such "textual silences" and "blind spots" of history tell us both about its makers and its writers.[18]

Interestingly, when non-Israeli historians, such as Conway and Gilbert, suggest that information about Auschwitz could have helped the Jews survive the Nazi atrocities, they are dismissed at once for accepting Vrba's testimony at face value or for being misled by him.[19] Such accusations are meant to insinuate that Conway, Gilbert, and others have lost their professional judgment in the face of Vrba's thesis, whereas the "objectivity" of the Israeli historians immunizes them against such a deficiency.[20]

This long-term tradition of discrediting seems to have affected even the eminent Czech Jewish historian Erich Kulka after he joined the Israeli establishment. Kulka, while still in Czechoslovakia, interviewed the Auschwitz escapees and wrote about them extensively and favorably, giving full recognition to their names and to their rare historical contribution.[21] After he immigrated to Israel and began writing under the aegis of Yad Vashem, Kulka seems to have adopted the position of clouding and discrediting.[22] Now he refers to Vrba as "Rosenberg-Vrba," and chooses to tell his Hebrew readers that, unlike other escapees, the critical position Vrba held vis-à-vis the members of the Working Group, who "saved and supported him," was not justified since they were, after all, good Zionists who lived and worked for more than thirty years in Israel. Kulka hopes that these letters will throw the "right light" on the events for the readers. He does not specify what exactly this "right light" might be.[23]

In May 1991, following an interview with Kulka, Ruth Davis, the editor of the *Newsletter of the Czechoslovak Jewish Communities,* heads one of her articles as follows: "Inside Auschwitz, Erich Kulka and Ota Kraus secretly documented the Nazi mass murders. Five escaped from the death camp *to take the news* to the outside world. Hungary halted deportations to Auschwitz." Throughout the newsletter she refers to Vrba exclusively as "Walter Rosenberg." Twelve years later, on October 6, 2003, she sent a copy of this newsletter to Vrba, with a letter in which she writes, among other things:

> Dear Prof. Vrba,
> I was walking out of Barnes & Nobles when I caught sight of a book on Auschwitz on display. The name Vrba caught my attention as possibly Czech, so I went to look at it. It is difficult to describe my amazement when I realized that "Vrba" is Rosenberg.
> As you see from the enclosed newsletter and publication, I heard the story of your escape from late Erich Kulka, and was profoundly impressed by what you attempted and achieved. *Kulka never mentioned to me that you are still living, or that you are in Canada.* He probably thought I knew it. . . ."[24]

To the misnaming, misreporting, miscrediting, one ought to add the discrepancy between the English and Hebrew writings of leading Israeli scholars. Thus, we find that the escape from Auschwitz falls within Bauer's studies on the Jewish–Nazi negotiations and Gutman's studies on Auschwitz. Whereas the escape of Vrba and Wetzler is widely mentioned in Bauer's 1994 and Gutman's 1994 publications in English, it is not given the same form of staging in their publications in Hebrew around this time.[25] This type of biased history, of course, is not exclusive to the Israeli scholars. It has long been documented by analysts of college history curricula that historians discuss certain historical events in a critical manner when they write for their peers but that they tend to adhere to the noncritical hegemonic narrative when they write for their students.[26] If the readers of history are regarded as the jury, as one analyst puts it, the historians' work resembles that of prosecuting attorneys who collate documents in search of discrepancies. "Unlike the jury, they have the privilege to actively question sources and delve into their conscious and unconscious motives. Since the reader, like a juror, is unable to question witnesses directly or subject them to cross examination, they tend to see the locus of authority in the text."[27] In this case, it is important to examine further not only "what the text says, but what it does."[28]

One version of the Vrba–Wetzler report is placed in a glass showcase at the entrance to the Yad Vashem library in the permanent exhibit of major documents from the Holocaust. But what guarantee do we have that with this form of staging the narrative itself will not remain hidden "beneath layers of national myths and explanations?"[29]

SEVEN

MISREPRESENTING

The non-publication of Vrba's memoirs in Hebrew for more than thirty-five years is apparently less disturbing to some Israeli Holocaust historians than any of the mistakes Vrba may have made, which they deem unforgivable. A glance at the kind of mistakes in question shows the following. Vrba is accused by Professor Bauer of, among other things, erroneously stating that "five months after he was deported, he still saw in Auschwitz the arrival of transports of Slovak Jews who were unaware of what was awaiting them." Bauer points out, "If he was deported on June 30, five months thereafter was November. But there were no transports from Slovakia in November."[1] This accusation is one among several intended to discredit Vrba's account of the facts and his right to an opinion on these facts. But a careful examination of the Auschwitz Calendar[2] suggests that Bauer is too hasty in the weight that he gives to Vrba's mistakes and disproportionate in measuring them. True, there were no transports in November, and Vrba made a mistake of about ten days. But there was no mistake about the idea he intended to convey—the ignorance of the prospective victims. Indeed, there was a transport some time after he was deported, not five but four months later. On October 21, 1942, 1,000 Slovak Jews arrived at Auschwitz. "Of them, 121 men (nos. 69073–69193) and 78 women (nos. 22801–22878) were selected for slave labor."[3] The rest were murdered.

Even if Vrba is off by ten days, this does not diminish the importance of the fundamental question that merits serious historical and perhaps moral consideration: Why were the deportees so ignorant of their destination, which by that time was known to the Jewish Council? Is a mistake of ten days, when recalling the transport after an interval of twenty years, a justifiable reason for banning the appearance in Hebrew of the memoirs of this Holocaust witness? Do Vrba's mistakes cause more historical confusion than the three versions of Krasniansky's testimony;[4] the two different versions of Freudiger's accounts of when he first saw the report;[5] Hanzi Brand's three versions of when Kasztner first saw the report;[6] and the version asserting Weissmandel's authorship of the report?[7] Yet none of these has had their name elided from Israeli reading lists on the Holocaust.

As Vrba notes in both versions of *The Preparations for the Holocaust in Hungary*, he finds his account subjected to further ongoing debate, this time not regarding any mistake but regarding his estimate of the number of those annihilated in Auschwitz (calculated through observation alone!) at 1,750,000;[8] this is deemed too high, or "an exaggerated statistics" as Bauer put it[9] though it precisely matches German figures.[10] Leading Israeli Holocaust historians put the number at 1,350,000.

But how is it that we find such a huge gap between the statistics and the narrative? Dan Diner remarks, "Auschwitz stands for a mode of murder that is standardized, serial annulling [of] individual biographies. In this sense 'Auschwitz' has statistics but no narrative. The figure of six million stands for this forfeiture of narrativity, and constant questioning of this figure reflects not so much a search for truth driven by a frenetic urge for exactitude as a coded interrogation of the event itself."[11]

As a center of documentation, Yad Vashem holds one of the most extensive collections of Holocaust documents. There is no Hebrew or English version of the Vrba-Wetzler report. The German version is marked M-20/153. But most interesting is the fate of the Hungarian version of the Vrba-Wetzler report, marked 015/9. This document is presented in the archive without the names of its authors and can be found only in a file that deals with the Kasztner's case![12] As indicated earlier, an inquiry from Yehoshua Ben Ami, the Hebrew translator of Vrba's memoirs, elicited this response from Yad Vashem: "Thank you for your letter of June 15, 1997. Indeed, it would have been important to translate the Vrba-Wetzler report, just as it is important to translate other significant documents. . . . Hopefully we will have the money one day."

In 1999, a year after Vrba's memoirs were at last published in Hebrew, an account of the escape from Auschwitz and of the Vrba-Wetzler report was finally included in Gutman's Hebrew writings for high school students (though no reference for Vrba's memoirs is made). This contained also a public acknowledgement of the blocking of the Vrba-Wetzler report: "Kasztner was given a copy of the report on 29 April 1944. . . . but at that time he had already made a decision, together with other Jewish leaders, choosing not to disseminate the report in order not to harm the negotiations with the Nazis."[13] As observed by Browning, even if the testimony of a survivor "did not achieve justice, it can still serve history."[14]

PART THREE

BETWEEN HISTORY AND MEMORY: VRBA QUESTIONS

What do you tell the dead when you lose?

J. W. DOWER

"The history of a society," says Jan T. Gross, "can be conceived as a collective biography. And just as in a biography—which is also composed of discrete episodes—everything in the history of a society is in rapport with everything else. And if at some point in this collective biography a big lie is situated, then everything that comes afterward will be devoid of authenticity and laced with fear of discovery."[1]

Drawing on testimony that emanated from the 1949 Polish trial, Gross meticulously describes how on July 10, 1941, good Polish citizens in the small village of Jedwabne terrorized and killed approximately 1,600 Jews who had been their neighbors for generations, although a monument in the village ascribes the massacre to the Germans. In his book, Gross, a Polish immigrant professor of politics and European studies at New York University, tries to place this heinous crime in historical and political context, concluding that he could explain but not fully understand and hoping that young Poles were ready to confront the unvarnished history of Polish–Jewish relations during the war. The book caused great consternation in Poland. His thesis was termed "hate speech," and letters were sent to Princeton University

Press urging it to consider withholding the publication of the book in English.

Like Gross, Arendt and Vrba clearly appear to be questioning the uniform messages that dominated their immediate past at a time when the postmodern dismantling of master narratives was barely on the horizon: How ought we relate to cooperating leaders? Mediating historians? Corrupt leaders? Powerful knowers?

The following chapters discuss the silence regarding these issues. And if silence is an admission of knowledge, argues Ernestine Schlant in her study of the post-Holocaust German literature, "then the paramount question is: What knowledge about the Holocaust is being repressed, denied, avoided, and how does this avoidance find expression?"[2]

EIGHT

COOPERATING LEADERS

"When systematic persecution of the Jews began," writes the father of George Soros,

> it was carried out not by the Germans, nor by their Hungarian lackeys, but—most astonishing—by the Jews themselves. . . . As Jews could not go to school any more and their teachers could not teach, they were ordered to report to council headquarters. The children were enlisted as couriers under the command of their teachers. My son, George, also became a courier. On the second day he returned home at seven in the evening. . . . he handed me a small slip of paper, with a typewritten message [that he was ordered to deliver to various addresses]: "SUMMONS You are requested to report tomorrow morning at 9 o'clock at the Rabbinical Seminary in Rokk Szilard Street. Please bring with you a blanket and food for two days. THE JEWISH COUNCIL."[1]

But is it indeed fair to pass judgment on the Jewish Councils in these hard times? After all, as a community without arms or a tradition of fighting their own rulers but rather of putting their trust in God, the Jewish Councils could not encourage resistance, nor would they have wanted to. Most councils were dominated by a long history, during which, particularly in Europe, the Jewish posture in the face of destruction was not shaped on the spur of the moment but through a tradition of passivity, compliance, attempts at bribery, and the like. Up-front resistance would not have prevented the deportations and would certainly have meant a definite death sentence to the council and swift and terrible collective punishment to all at the hands of the Germans. As summarized by Langer, the satanic Nazi plot enabled the Jewish Council to decide how they would want to destroy themselves, a position that hardly resembled a choice.[2]

From the Auschwitz ramp, Vrba is quick to share Hilberg's conclusion that the Judenrate's position marks a form of collaboration. From her Manhattan apartment, Arendt is more hesitant and would rather have us understand this behavior as a form of cooperation.

Both Arendt and Vrba share the view that full responsibility for the Jewish destruction lay with the Nazis. Yet, both Arendt and Vrba see a rather simple escape from this plot: If the informed "sheep" had scattered, the organized slaughter the Germans had planned would have been disrupted. Both would agree that the Eichmann trial required historiographical radicalism and that it failed to teach a revolutionary lesson for the future.[3]

And what was the fate of individual radical voices at the time of the Eichmann controversy? Vrba was still an unknown hero and thus could easily be suppressed.

Arendt's voice was suppressed as well, but it could not be dismissed. She herself became the subject of a severe public attack for her faulty understanding of Eichmann and her merciless condemnations of the Jews. And she was blamed for the offensive tone of her criticism (for example, when referring to the Judenrate as bearers of secrets and to Rabbi Leo Baeck in particular as the "Jewish Fuhrer"). Residing in her Manhattan apartment, she was made out to be not only ignorant of Jewish history but also incapable of understanding the complexity of the situation—a claim that thirty years later would be directed at Vrba.

The accusations brought against Arendt were widely published in Hebrew. Arendt did, of course, respond to her critics, but this response was kept from the Hebrew reader for almost 40 years:

There was no people and no group in Europe which reacted differently under the immediate pressure of terror. The question I raised was that of the cooperation of Jewish functionaries during the "Final Solution," and this question is so very uncomfortable because one cannot claim that they were traitors. (There were traitors, too, but that is irrelevant.) In other words, until 1939 and even until 1941, whatever Jewish functionaries did or did not do is understandable and excusable. Only later does it become highly problematical. This issue came up during the trial and it was of course my duty to report it. This constitutes our part of the so-called "unmastered past," and although you may be right that it is too early for a "balanced judgment" (though I doubt this), I do believe that we shall only come to terms with this past if we begin to judge and to be frank about it. I have made my own position plain, and yet it is obvious that you did not understand it. I said that there was no possibility of resistance, but there existed the possibility of *doing nothing*.[4]

The hegemonic reading often conveys the message of the good intention of these moral hostages: "the Judenrat reinforced the Jews' power of endurance in their struggle for survival,"[5] and in many cases they tried to delay the administrative and economic measures that the Germans were imposing, or at least to alleviate them.[6] According to Diner, "The Judenrat tried to gain more time, or to protract the period of 'borrowed time' allotted them by the Nazis, by expanding their sole asset: the physical labor power at their disposal . . . the strategy aimed at gaining precious time made it necessary for the Judenrat to make decisions in keeping with the logic of utilitarian considerations."[7]

According to Saul Friedlander, the attitude and the response of the Jewish Councils and the passivity of the Jewish population are topics that are doomed never to be fully investigated because they "are studied almost solely *within* the groups directly involved. . . . in this case, the massive impact of collective memory on historiography is not even countered by different perspectives stemming from the different existential fields of the historians involved." These self-serving accounts, naturally, are limited, given that historical narrative is an insufficient container or organizer for traumatic experiences.[8]

We recall that on Vrba and Wetzler's arrival, Oskar Neumann, the head of the Jewish Council, instructed his staff to verify the escapees'

knowledge and identities against the existing lists of the Slovakian deportees. Though at the time he was a member of the Jewish Council,
we have no data about his exact role in the forced deportations. The *Encyclopedia of the Holocaust* assigned the formal blame to the head of the
Jewish Council during the deportation, Sebestyen. His leadership, we
are told, "lacked courage and vision . . . [he was] not prepared to act in
defiance of orders." Does this mean that not all members of the Jewish
Council were obedient? If so, who were not, and how would we assess
to what extent? A vague answer is provided when the text goes on *"the
rest of the center followed his lead."*[9] Was Dr. Neumann part of the "rest
of the center?"

Neumann's memoirs, *Im Schatten des Todes,* provide a different account.[10] He argues that he and some other activists disagreed with the
line taken by the center. It is uncertain (at least, it was for those on the
deportation list) how he could maintain his position in the Jewish center while opposing the deportations as they were happening and how,
in the end, he won the election as head of the Judenrat in 1943. After
all, the Judenrat was "an institution set up by the Nazis and active under its supervision and at its bidding."[11]

In fact, we are missing information about three types of lists that
were compiled by the Judenrat. First, the list of those who were *definitely* going to be deported; second, the list of those who *might* be deported (in case there was a need to enlarge the quota); and, third, the
list of those who were definitely *exempted* from deportation. Which list
ought historians to represent when they describe the past? What voice
will they silence in their concern about the future? Are we to accept that
there are tales of "history without people"?[12]

These questions might sustain David Lowenthal's argument that history is both less and more than the past. It is less than the past because
"it is impossible to recover or recount more than a tiny fraction of what
has taken place, and no historical account ever corresponds precisely
with any actual past. Three things limit what can be known: the immen-
sity of the past itself, the distinction between past events and accounts
of those events, and the invisibility of bias—especially presenting

bias." It is more than the past because "knowing the future of the past forces the historian to shape his account to come out as things have done. . . . he must use what he knows in telling history. . . . The very process of communication demands creative change to make the past convincing and intelligible. Like memory, history conflates, compresses, exaggerates."[13] And, we may add, obliterates.

The Slovak Jewish Council is presented, by way of apologia, as providing only *"technical and secretarial help"* (to the Nazis) and the reader is reminded that "the [deportation] lists were supplied by Slovak authorities."[14] How should we go about judging these technical and secretarial helpers?

A similar form of apologia is presented in the case of the fleeing Freudiger, who smuggled out his entire family with the help of a senior SS officer, leaving behind a puzzled community. Robinson describes this behavior as follows: "He [Freudiger] *left* Hungary for Romania" And sees this departure as having a "reason [which is] *very simple*":

> Mr. Freudiger left Budapest on August 10, 1944. By that time all the Jews in Hungary outside Budapest had already been deported to Auschwitz and the Budapest Jews had been reassured by the Hungarian ruler Horthy (and they believed in the firmness of his decision) that no more deportations would take place, as indeed they did not before Szalasi came to power. Freudiger himself left at the *suggestion* of Wisliceny, who warned him that Eichmann intended to deport him and his family.[15]

Robinson was adviser to Gideon Hausner, the Attorney General in the Eichmann trial—the above passage appears in his response to the detached position from which Arendt criticizes the wartime Jewish leaders.

A similar form of writing history without (the ordinary) people is also found in the writings of Andreas Biss, who helped to construct the list of names for Kasztner's train. Biss, a colleague of Kasztner and a cousin of Brand, is widely quoted as a source by historians who study the destruction of Hungarian Jewry. He explains the intricate compilation of the deportation list in a way that is echoed in many other writings about the Jewish Council. Biss writes that when he found familiar names of "*a good many persons*" on the deportations list, "other names were inserted in their place, in part on the orders of the Hungarian, German or Jewish chiefs of this ghetto. It is hardly surprising that this Dante-esque tragedy gave rise to feelings of bitterness and hatred—still lively today—among those whose close relations were not allowed on this test convoy."[16] Biss further provides the moral rationale for the Judenrat's decision to conceal the Vrba-Wetzler report: "It was part of Clages' job . . . to keep an eye on Eichmann and to see that everything was done to ensure that the secret behind the 'final solution' should be completely guarded. *It was therefore necessary that the object of the deportations should remain unknown.*"[17]

With the exception of Gizi Fleischmann, most of the Jewish leaders from the Slovakian Jewish community survived the war. Most of the (non-affiliated) Jews from that community, however, disappeared. As a result, there is an inevitable asymmetry in the documentation on which historians rely. Rothkirchen, for example, writes: "Fortunately, the majority of the Slovak Jewish leaders survived the war, and, thus, aside from the plethora of correspondence clandestinely forwarded to the free world, they were able to write down their reminiscences."[18]

Vrba is not alone in feeling apart from the hegemonic narrative of the Slovak community. In his 1997 book, *I Did Not Want to Be a Jew*, Juraj Spitzer provides the reader with some of the feelings of the uninformed deportees, even though he himself was protected by the Slovak Judenrat.

> It was suspected that the primary concern of its officers was their own rescue. Hope and powerlessness led to hate against the Jewish officials, because they were unable to prove themselves successful against the perpetrators of liquidation. The special department of the Center for Jews *unwillingly* became an organ of the liquidators, and it is questionable whether all the legal means, interventions, and illegal bribes brought about the anticipated results—or whether the whole thing was not an illusion, albeit sincere, in its attempt to rescue people.[19]

The language used to describe the wartime Jewish leadership is often couched in sterile, moral-free, scientific, and sophisticated terms, thus more concealing than revealing.[20]

- The Slovakian Judenrat, thus, was neither preparing lists nor was it involved in favoritism. It only provided the authorities with the *"statistical breakdown of the Jewish population."*
- The fact that the leaders had to comply with the Nazis, albeit unwillingly, has to be inferred from the description of their position as involving a *"dual role."*
- In the Nazi scheme of things, the Jewish leaders were kept as moral hostages: The Jewish leaders were often the last to leave for Auschwitz. Knowing that their day would come, they naturally pinned their hopes on an Allied victory in time to save them from the fate of their less fortunate brethren. But this is not an easy topic to discuss "since Nazi extermination policy depended to a certain measure on the fortune of war, there existed an unknown *war coefficient*—the "time element."[21]
- "Here [in Hungary] the protocol acquired some kind of publication. It was taken to heads of churches and leaders, *but it was not distributed among the Jewish communities generally* [sic], even though this was May [1944], the time when they were being deported to Auschwitz."[22]
- "It is beyond question: The Auschwitz Protocols did reach the Jewish Council and Zionist activists, including the Halutz Underground. *Yet they did not transmit this information to the Jewish public when the deportation began.*"[23]
- "The report remained *unknown to the Jewish population inside Hungary itself.*"[24]

Porat confirms: "Perhaps they did not know in the sense that the information did not become an internalized awareness, because human beings tend to believe that someone else, not they, is endangered, even when evidence to the contrary is visible. . . . Perhaps in Budapest Jews knew and heard more, but in the more far-flung areas of the country, in the small towns, *only the activists knew.*"[25] But what did the informed do with their knowledge? Dr. Imre Kertesz, the 2002 Nobel Laureate for Literature, recollects: "People belonging to an organization called *The Jewish Council* who could be recognized by the band they wore on their arm, said that, anyway, sooner or later, willingly or unwillingly, all the people who were assembled at the brick factory would be transferred to Germany and that those who volunteered first would be given the better places. Furthermore, they would benefit from traveling on a wagon with 60 people which later would have to hold at least 80 people as there was a shortage of trains, as they explained to everybody. Therefore, there was no point in hesitating, and that is what I thought."[26]

NINE

RESISTING INDIVIDUALS

"History," as suggested by Claude Levi-Strauss, "is never only 'history of'" [but] "is always also 'history for,' not only in the sense that it is narrated with a certain ideological aim but also that it is narrated for a specific public." How ought the historian to have told this heroic Holocaust tale?

This question is not a new one in the case of national histories. These, as Levi-Strauss further explains, "are intended first and foremost for individuals and groups that make up the collective 'we.' It is also from within that 'organic' community of memory that pleas for historicization originate, again to accommodate its own needs."[1]

In an attempt to structure a collective "we," both Israeli and Communist historians appear to employ a process of collectivization of the escape narrative, a position shared as well as by Auschwitz survivors who stayed behind the Iron Curtain during the writing of their memoirs.

Under the pseudonym Lanik, Wetzler wrote his account in the form of a novel told in the third person.[2] Both Vrba and Wetzler discuss their arrest, arrival in Auschwitz, Himmler's visit and, obviously, the escape and the report. But Wetzler's fictional version departs from Vrba's account in its collective flavor. In his book, Lanik narrates the escape as a Russian enterprise. In keeping with the Communists' desired understanding of the Holocaust victims and their liberators, the informants are Russian, the audience is Communist Party members, and there is no mention that the victims are Jews. Paradoxically, the non-Jewish Russian prisoners were not allowed to work on the ramp and their knowledge of the camp statistics was minimal.[3]

As Lanik elaborates, on their journey the escapees met a working-class Pole called Tadeusz who gave them an address in Slovakia and assured them: "The Communists helped you in Poland, they will also help you at home!"[4] Vrba disagrees with this version, as he states that during their journey from Auschwitz to Slovakia they never asked names or gave their names. Lanik recounts that members of the Hlinka Guard (who became Communists after the war) helped the fugitives. They took the escapees directly to the Communist Party in Zilina, not to the Jewish Council. Though Vrba acknowledged meeting with the Communist Party much later after their escape from Auschwitz, he saw no relevance mentioning this in his writings as no help was offered to the escapees (viewed as either Jews, non-proletarian, or "bourgeois") from this quarter.

Before their escape, Vrba and Wetzler made endless efforts to learn about the methods of mass killing in Auschwitz. Vrba, for example, made contact with a prisoner named Filip Muller who became one of his most valuable sources of information: "Filip stoked the furnaces in the crematorium. By the amount of fuel made available, he could reckon how many bodies were to be burned because the S.S. never wasted fuel by overloading their fires."[5] According to Lanik, they wrote a report based on statistics of killing, making six copies which they hid in a metal pipe they carried out of Auschwitz, along with the drawings of the camp and a Zyklon B container label. Muller in his own memoir, confirmed Wetzler's account of the delivery to the escapees of a label from a canister of Zyklon B gas as well as other information. Vrba's version disagrees with this. He states categorically that in escaping from the camp he refused to take any notes, and the entire report was produced from memory. Lanik seems to corroborate this when his narrator relates how the Germans shot at them during the escape, and he realized that the pipe containing the statistics had disappeared. He concludes, "Dear Vasil, all your work is lost." Oskar Krasniansky himself gave additional support for Vrba's testimony seventeen years later.

On February 15, 1961, while serving in an official Israeli position in Cologne, Germany, Krasniansky vividly recalled transcribing their words. In a deposition he gave under oath for the Eichmann's trial, he stated: "I locked myself with them in a room and I wrote down from their own mouths the report. . . . due to their wonderful memory."[6] One can further ask how, if their knowledge relied heavily on prepared notes, which were lost, were they able to tell such an accurate story after eleven days of dangerous travel?

Vrba's connection with the resistance within Auschwitz is well documented.[7] In his own memoirs he acknowledges the help he received: "It put me in touch with an element in camp life which I never dreamed existed: a powerful underground movement, without whose help I could never have escaped."[8] Historians and others have often cited this help as an indication that Vrba and Wetzler were emissaries of the underground. Cohen, for example, insists that the two "delivered" the information from Auschwitz, as if it had been collected by someone else.[9] Paradoxically, it is Herman Langbein, a former fighter in the Spanish Civil War and head of the Communist underground in Auschwitz at the time of the escape and regarded as a highly credible writer, who seems to contradict the Israeli–Communist "collective deliverance" logic. Langbein refutes the idea that the escapees were the underground emissaries. He clearly indicates that Vrba never obtained any knowledge about the mass extermination going on in Birkenau from the Communist organization. In fact, the situation was the reverse: The knowledge that the organization had was provided by Vrba.[10]

How ought Israeli historians to have dealt with the escapees' narratives? After all, none of the escapees had even a minimal layer of Zionist veneer: Lederer escaped with the help of a Nazi! Vrba and Wetzler and Mordowicz and Rosin did not define themselves, necessarily, as Zionist escapees, nor were they emissaries of a Zionist resistance group.

In the early years of the state of Israel, the concept of resistance during the Holocaust was narrowly defined as "any *group* action consciously taken in opposition to known or surmised laws, actions, or

intentions directed against the Jews by the Germans and their sup-
porters."[11] Given this definition, one can understand the problematic
categorization of the escape from Auschwitz. At the 1968 Yad Vashem
conference on Jewish Resistance, Rothkirchen argued that the source
of information that reached the Working Group came "from refugees
and the first escapees from concentration camps who reached Slovakia.
The Working Group collected testimony regarding the process of the
exterminations and the death camps and passed this on to the free world
together with its own call and warning. These reports reached their des-
tinations. They are to be found in various archives in the world."[12]
When Professor Kulka, who had studied the heroic resistance action of
the five escapees from Auschwitz, evinced surprise at that conference
that their part in informing the Working Group was missing from
Rothkirchen's presentation, she answered, "I was speaking of the *organized* escapes. The escapes from Auschwitz were acts of *individual* heroism" (p. 436, emphasis added). Kulka's suggestion that the escapees
should be recognized on the national level, was rejected on the ground
that "Yad Vashem Honored only people who resisted with weapons."[13]

As we know now, Vrba's and Wetzler's escape from Auschwitz and
their report led neither to the direct bombing of the railway line to
Auschwitz nor to a dramatic uprising in Hungary but rather to a fairly
ponderous diplomatic chain of events that ended with the halting of the
deportation. Yet outside Israel their escape is often viewed as a seminal
event. D. A. Brugioni, for example, writes: "the information about
Auschwitz provided by two escapees, Rudolf Vrba and Alfred Wetzler,
was never made available to those interpreting the Farben plant photos.
It is my professional opinion that had such information been provided
to the interpreters they would have quickly located the gas chambers
and the crematoria."[14] But in Israel, as Diner remarks, "despite all tem-
poral distance, the past still stubbornly retains its immediacy and con-
temporaneity resists becoming history. It is thus no surprise that all
discourse on history in Israel is *ipso facto* discourse of legitimacy."[15]
Could a narrative of an individualistic escape, by a non–Zionist Jew,
critical of his Jewish leaders, ever be made to harmonize with the "collective aura" that dominated the state of Israel?[16]

How could he ever be part of the Israeli "narrative strategy" of identity?[17] How could he ever belong to the "imagined community" of the Jewish State?[18] Similar questions surrounded the case of Dr. Mark Edelman, one of the leaders of the Warsaw uprising, a member of the Bund and Jewish Polish Nationalist. His book *The Ghetto Is Fighting*, first published in 1945, was translated into Hebrew only fifty-six years later, in 2001. Like Vrba, Edelman never "ascended" to Israel, refusing to become the "dead and obedient hero who could be molded along with the political order of that time. On the contrary he remained alive and kicking and refusing and, therefore, extremely inconvenient for the creation of a heroic Zionist condensing and compensating myth."[19] Responding with a highly positive letter of recommendation to its Senate when the University of Haifa was considering awarding Vrba an honorary doctorate, one of the Israeli historians who was approached could not help but add: "Vrba did not manage to settle down in Israel."[20] In fact, after having resided for a short time in Israel, Vrba *chose* to live elsewhere: first in England and later in Canada. Likewise, Wetzler ended up back in Slovakia, Mordowicz in Canada, and Rosin in Germany. If being home means being acknowledged, Israel was not their home.

TEN

MEDIATING HISTORIANS

After the war, all five of the Jewish Auschwitz fugitives found themselves living behind the Iron Curtain. Vrba was the only one who
pursued academic studies, earning a doctoral degree in biochemistry
from the University of Prague. He also was the only one to escape again
from a totalitarian regime, this time by defecting from a Czechoslovak
scientific delegation to the West with the help of a former Auschwitz
inmate in the Czechoslovak administration. He lived in Israel for a year
and a half (1958–1960), working as a biochemist at the Israeli Institute
for Veterinary Medicine in Beit Dagon. During his stay he even had the
opportunity to see Oskar Neumann, who was once again in a position
of leadership—now in the Czechoslovak immigrants' organization in
Israel—and to have dinner with him at Mr. Krasniansky's home. Soon
afterward, the latter would testify at Eichmann's trial about the nameless escapees. Subsequently Vrba continued his academic research and
teaching at various medical institutions in England, the United States,
and Canada.

All the escapees provided some sort of testimony, not always in complete agreement with one another or necessarily with the historians'
accounts. Kulka, for example, who wrote a novel based on Lederer's
account, was later blamed by Lederer for "many untruths and errors."[1]

Most Israeli Holocaust historians have opted to belittle Vrba's legit-
imate questioning as to whether an increase in the number of better informed citizens would have disrupted the deportations. Instead, Vrba
is charged with disrupting the logic of the events, as follows: First, he

is not a historian.[2] Second, he has no right to try to convince the historians that the Working Group were, in fact, collaborating with the Nazis at some point.[3] Third, he ought to understand that "the Working Group knew that the truth about the extermination was already known" and therefore did not disseminate the report in their community. Fourth, he and Wetzler "could have disseminated their testimony themselves."[4] Fifth, Vrba is simply a bitter victim who refuses to accept that resistance was not an option.[5] Sixth, he has no right to criticize those leaders who had previously helped numerous refugees. Seventh, because Vrba is a non-Zionist, his testimony can never be as credible as Neumann's.[6] But were Vrba's ideas and concerns so different from those raised by a Zionist heroine named Hanna Szenes?

On March 13, 1944, when Vrba was still in Auschwitz planning his escape, and one week before the Germans invaded Hungary, three Jews from Palestine (Hanna Szenes and two men named Joel Palgi and Peretz Goldstein) parachuted into Yugoslavia to assist British intelligence efforts. All three had parents and other close friends and relatives living in Hungary.[7] "The mission, it was envisioned, would provide advice about and leadership for the organization of some kind of resistance and self-help in the event of German occupation."[8] The parachutists were expected to radio back to British headquarters military information that could be helpful in defeating the Nazis. On June 9, 1944 (the Vrba-Wetzler report had not yet surfaced in Budapest), Szenes crossed the border into Hungary with the aim of organizing resistance.[9] She was captured right away. Her fellow parachutists Palgi and Goldstein crossed the border a few days later and managed to get to Budapest. All three infiltrators had been given Kasztner's name prior to their departure, and now the two men tried to approach him for assistance. But Kasztner was engaged in negotiations over the release of the train (which would eventually leave on June 30), and he must have found it problematic to be asked to represent British-sponsored Jewish spies while in the midst of those negotiations.[10] In the end, both were picked up by the political police and were destined for deportation. Palgi succeeded in escaping and later presented love–hate testimony on behalf of Kasztner at his trial in Israel. Goldstein died in a concentration camp, unaware that his own parents were among the prominent Jews on Kasztner's train.

Hanna Szenes, who was born in Budapest, had emigrated to Palestine before the war and settled at Kibbutz Sdot Yam, near Caesarea. After her capture in Hungary, the Hungarian police, in their attempt to compel her to cooperate, arrested her widowed mother, Katherine Szenes. Until then Szenes's mother was sure that her daughter was safe and well in Palestine. Mother and daughter were held in two separate cells for three months. Szenes refused to tell her captors her transmitter code and did not give in to the threats against her mother's life. After five months in prison, on November 7, 1944, the twenty-three-year-old Szenes was put on trial by a Nyilas court, where she proudly defended herself; but she was condemned to the firing squad. Her mother emigrated to Israel after the war. She would later provide one of the most dramatic testimonies at the Kasztner's trial, describing how he had failed to help her, despite his numerous connections in Budapest.[11]

As a "symbol of courage, steadfastness and moral strength," "virginal Szenes" is one of the most commemorated Holocaust symbols in Israel.[12] Although the mission was a complete failure, it is believed that "the bravery of the parachutists had a positive influence on many of the Zionist Pioneers and unaffiliated younger Jewish intellectuals who had become disillusioned with the [Jewish] leadership."[13] In Israeli historiography, Szenes is described as a passionate Zionist, a woman with a romantic and sensitive soul and a great interest in literature and poetry, who came from a bourgeois assimilationist background. Her trial became the inspiration for numerous theatrical narratives in Israel.[14]

In the 1990 *Encyclopedia of the Holocaust*, Szenes's bravery and wisdom are associated with her wish to "*organize [the] resistance*" of Hungarian Jews.[15] Vrba's escape from Auschwitz was identical in mission. Like Szenes, he refused to accept that Jews ought to go like sheep to the gas chambers, believing that information could make a difference. While escaping he dreamed "of warning the Hungarians, of rousing them, of raising an army one million strong, an army that would fight rather than die."[16] But while Vrba and Szenes were alike in their ambition as well as in their strategy, only Szenes's narrative is described as a tale of heroism. Her idea of resistance is glorified. She is never labeled "a young Hungarian girl." Vrba and Wetzler's fundamental contribution to saving the Budapest Jews is not made clear, whereas Szenes's failure to save even one single Jew is not discussed. Vrba's idea of resistance, namely that informed Jews would hesitate to board the trains to Auschwitz, is uniformly dismissed as an unrealistic, insignificant, too simplistic, or inapplicable idea in the face of the unique setting of the Hungarian community.[17] Thus, it could happen that in the Israeli "popular consciousness" Szenes is glorified for her "blind patriotism" while Vrba is scolded for his "constructive patriotism."[18] Is Dawidowicz right when she argues this above form of "strategic remembering" is a matter of group pride rather than historical truth?[19]

Diner argues that "particular histories [were] implicitly denied via a kind of mere retelling according to the given national patterns. Particular narratives are reauthored, submerged and thereby hegemonalized."[20] This is often done by the political elite "to brush aside questions of the war's morality."[21]

An interesting parallel is found in the case of the canonical 1961 book of Raul Hilberg (*The Destruction of the European Jews*), which was never translated into Hebrew.[22] Scholars agree that Hilberg "has done more than any other single scholar to compile and analyze the facts of the Holocaust."[23] His work has been called a "monumental, brilliant, and, in my view, unsurpassed analysis of the Nazi bureaucracy."[24] Researchers share the idea that "to this day, there is no single work (certainly not written by an individual author) which supersedes this masterpiece of comprehensive historical research."[25]

In Michman's comprehensive book on the Holocaust (*Ha-Sho'ah ve-hikrah*), he tells readers that Hilberg's book "was translated into various languages—but not into Hebrew!" Although he points this out thirty-seven years after the publication of the English version, Michman does not explain to his Hebrew readers why Hilberg's book is still shunned by the Israeli establishment. But some indication follows: "When we analyze the activities of the Judenrat, we can identify two positions: one, which can be defined as 'Hilberg's position' . . . which sees the Judenrat as a Nazi instrument; the other can be defined as the 'Trunk-Weiss position' . . . which emphasizes the positive aspect of the Judenrat due to the organizational role that they took upon themselves in serving the community."[26]

In this context, it is illuminating to compare the representation of Vrba's narrative with that of others in the Holocaust discourse. Szenes received a whole entry in the 1990 *Encyclopedia of the Holocaust*. Vrba and Wetzler are mentioned under the entry "Auschwitz" and "The Auschwitz Protocols." Arendt received an entry as well (Arendt's Controversy[!]), but it contains no explanation of why her book had not been translated into Hebrew.

A change would occur, however, when two young Israeli-born artists, tried to search for a different version of the truth. The two had to file a lawsuit in 1998 against the Israeli government for permission to make a documentary film about Eichmann's trial, one of the few trials in history that had been filmed completely. They obtained permission; however, it turned out that this valuable footage had been stored in unsuitable conditions in Jerusalem, and two-thirds of it had already been destroyed due to humidity and lack of care over the years. From what survived, the two artists constructed a unique movie about Eichmann titled *The Specialist*. They chose to highlight all the aspects in Eichmann's testimony that reflected Hanna Arendt's thesis of Eichmann's not unique but banal evil. Shocked by the boycott of Arendt's book in Israel, the two filmmakers seem to have broken the thirty-five–year policy of suppression: Two years later, *Eichmann in Jerusalem* was published for the first time in Hebrew by Bavel. Yad Vashem is not connected in any way with the appearance of this edition.

And what was Yad Vashem's connection to the translation of Hilberg's book? In 1957 Hilberg was promised that Yad Vashem would publish his book in collaboration with Columbia University Press. At that time, the head of Yad Vashem's scientific section was Joseph Melkman, a noted Dutch historian and a Bergen Belsen survivor who had lost most of his family there. Soon thereafter, Melkman wrote to him that Yad Vashem was withdrawing its promise; it was problematic to accept a manuscript that was based on German documentation and highlighted Jewish submissiveness.

Hilberg was rather taken aback by this action. For him, Yad Vashem's greater emphasis on glorifying Jewish heroism than on the destruction wrought upon them by the Nazis resulted in an artificial setting and went against historical reality. Melkman rejected Hilberg's response and assured him that "we [at Yad Vashem] are not chauvinist zealots who reject a serious work based on such arguments."[27] By the exclamation sign Michman inserts when indicating that Hilberg's book was translated into numerous languages but not into Hebrew, he hints at criticism but refrains from telling his readers that Dr. Melkman was his father.

ELEVEN

CORRUPT SAVIORS

"I know an ending at which you would grow pale from envy, not a particularly happy one," writes Jurek Becker in his highly challenging book on the last days of the Lodz ghetto, *Jacob the Liar.* "I have fabricated it over the course of the years. I said to myself, it is really a crying shame that such a beautiful story would come so wretchedly to nothing. Invent an ending for it that can be halfway satisfying, one that is logical. A proper ending will atone for some of its shortcomings. Besides, all of them have earned a better end, not just Jacob."[1]

On June 7, 1944, secret radio listeners spread the word of D-Day in the Lodz ghetto. The message may have been made up, but we know it had a significant impact on the people's morale. It was imprinted on the mind of Jurek Becker, a seven-year-old ghetto inhabitant who later grew up in East Germany and initially wrote his story as a film script. Becker's fictional hero concocts a report of the advancing Russian troops as if broadcast over a nonexistent radio in his cellar in the Lodz ghetto. He hopes thereby to sustain the community's spirit until the liberation. In the book he suggests two endings for the historical event.

On September 8, 1939, at Lodz, Chaim Mordechai Rumkowski was appointed chairman of the Lodz Jewish Council by the occupying Germans. He was given a wide range of powers concerning day-to-day life, and a Jewish ghetto police force was organized and placed at his disposal. Rumkowski turned the ghetto into an enterprise with 120 factories that provided the Germans with slave labor and the Jews with basic food for their survival. He supervised these factories with great zeal and with a tyrannical hand. Rumkowski's policy was to keep the Jews alive by transforming them into a productive source of labor. He loved "his Jews" and he loved his power; under the Nazi aegis he printed postage stamps bearing his own likeness and with the help of the Nazis introduced a currency named after himself, the rmsks.[2] Like all other Nazi-appointed Jewish leaders, Rumkowski was put in an impossible situation: He was expected to fill in the names for the assigned quotas for the death transports leaving the ghetto of Lodz. "Rumkowski, then over 70, was a brutal dictator" writes Bauer. He knew about Auschwitz before anyone else in the Lodz ghetto, yet he tried to prevent the information from spreading in the ghetto. He allowed no food to be smuggled to the ghetto; he suppressed every stirring of Jewish resistance; he forced Jews into slave labor. . . . Of all the men who served on Jewish Councils during the Holocaust years, *Rumkowski probably was the nearest thing to a major war criminal.*"[3] Rumkowski's rule became the subject of controversy among historians and survivors alike.[4] Did he do enough to keep the Jews alive? By cooperating with the Nazis, did he make it easier for them to send the Lodz Jews to their deaths?

When in January 1942 Rumkowski was ordered to select 20,000 Jews from the Lodz ghetto for "resettlement," he succeeded in reducing the number to 10,000 and the Germans left the individual selections up to him. They had no doubt that he would carry out these orders as faithfully as he had carried out others. Rumkowski warned the fearful crowd: "Whoever opposes me will be arrested. . . . this action will be carried out." When Rumkowski had to construct a deportation list, he decided that the most humane way was to include the following: (1) 2,000 refugees from the provincial towns ("they would be happier in more familiar surroundings"); (2) the families of those men sent outside the ghetto for slave labor ("they would have a better chance of being reunited with their menfolk"); (3) the families on relief (their "resettlement" would enable productive workers to get more food); (4) criminals (those whose names appeared on the Central Card Index as having shown lack of obedience in the ghetto or who had been arrested for any reason whatsoever, from knocking over a garbage can to stealing a piece of wood for fuel); and (5) anyone who had ever been an enemy of Rumkowski.[5]

Yet evasion was possible. Corrupt as Rumkowski's bureaucracy was,

> when it came to keeping lists of names and addresses it was efficient. . . . Only the luckless with no "protection" were taken. The doctors examined the selected deportees to determine their "fitness for travel.". . . Rumkowski assured the Jews left behind that the deportees were going out to places where they would do agricultural work. At the loading platforms there were no bloody scenes, as in Warsaw; all went smoothly. The deportations started on January 15 and ended on January 29, 1942, when the quota was reached. A total of 10,103 were sent out "for resettlement." The deportees reached their final destination at Chelmno. None returned.[6]

By the summer of 1944 the Lodz ghetto was the only major ghetto in Poland—all the others had been liquidated. Its inhabitants might have obtained some knowledge from a hidden radio carrying reports on German defeats. When Rumkowski was ordered by the Germans to send more deportees, he used all his powers of persuasion to assure the workers that deportation did not mean death. He was helped by the classic Nazi perfidy: postcards received from the "resettled" people, instructions about careful labeling of baggage to avoid misdirection, and advice on what to take. Though he knew that all the deportees were going to be liquidated in Auschwitz, Rumkowski went about urging people to volunteer for the transports, saying that workers were needed in Germany to replace the Germans taken for the army.

One of his last orders, dated August 24, 1944, told the ghetto inhabitants to make sure that all the electric lights were turned off in the homes and factories they left, so that Allied planes would not be guided to bomb Lodz. Seven hundred men and women were left behind in the ghetto as clean-up gangs. They were mostly intellectuals under the special protection of Rumkowski. He could have stayed behind with them, but he chose not to. "Seeing his family going on the last train on August 30, 1944, [Rumkowski] asked to leave with them."[7] Many have hailed Rumkowski as a hero who did the best he could leading his community through the worst of circumstances. In the year 2000, however, Holocaust survivor Lucile Eichengreen stepped forward to provide testimony and research intending to show that Rumkowski was an abuser of power as well as a pedophile.[8]

There are two possible endings to Rumkowski's tale, one of which might be related to Vrba and Wetzler's escape from Auschwitz. As a result of the Vrba-Wetzler report, as well as other related factors, Horthy stopped the deportation of the Budapest Jews. If for some reason Horthy had not halted the deportation, history and memory might have had a different ending. The ovens at Birkenau would have consumed the rest of the Hungarian Jews (more than 200,000 souls) and would have been too overworked to devour the Lodz ghetto people as well. Had there been no escape from Auschwitz and had several thousand inhabitants of the Lodz ghetto survived in the end, Rumkowski would have turned out a Judenrat hero. The idea was raised as early as 1973. Bauer writes:

> By handing over a certain number of Jews on command, he [Rumkowski] hoped to save the rest. The gamble very nearly worked. The Lodz ghetto survived longer than any other in Poland; when the SS sought to liquidate it, the Army, needing uniforms, postponed the plan. As of July 1944, 68,000 of Lodz's 250,000 Jews were still alive and working as slaves. The Soviet forces were then less than sixty miles away, but, for reasons of their own, they stopped their advance and in August all but eight hundred of the city's Jews were sent to their death. When the Soviets resumed their attack in January 1945, they took Lodz within three days. If they had come a few months earlier, liberating 68,000 Jews instead of 800, *might not Rumkowski, despite all his crimes, have been hailed as a hero?*[9]

TWELVE

POWERFUL KNOWERS

On October 23, 1943, in a transport from Bergen Belsen, an unknown woman, one among many other unknown women who were being led to the gas chambers, decided to act on the vague knowledge she had of their impending fate and "pulled a pistol out of the hands of an SS man and shot two others, Oberscharfuhrer Schillinger and Unterscharfuhrer Emmerich."[1] This individual act triggered resistance among the other women—a resistance that ended with a different type of death for them. Instead of being shoved into the gas chambers, they were killed by an SS reinforcement that was always kept ready for this kind of situation. If information "benefited" individuals whose death was imminent, could it not have benefited these individuals one stage earlier?

One need be neither a historian nor a psychologist to realize that in a crisis situation individuals and groups who lack information hold a position inferior to those who have information. During the Nazi extermination, all that was needed was for one to stand daily at the ramp at Auschwitz, waiting for the transports of arriving deportees to come in. From this vantage point one could observe the Germans' greatest fear: the disaster of "informed" deportees. Despite knowing that the victims had long been exposed to extreme conditions, were arriving after several days of being shipped in boxcars, without food, water, air, and proper sanitation, the Germans nevertheless feared resistance. They were fully aware that, even if resistance was not successful, it could slow down the process of mass murder. They were aware that knowledge is power.

98

Throughout the eight months of his assignment in "Canada," Vrba took note of incidents that threatened to upset the simple but powerful efficiency of the SS system of silencing. The first concerned 3,000 French Jews who arrived on a cold night in 1942. Men, women, and children were queuing obediently for selection when something went wrong.

> Every night a truck, carrying a harvest of dead from Auschwitz to Birkenau, passed at right angles to the head of the ramp. Normally nobody saw what it held and it was gone before anyone could even think about it; but that night it was overloaded. That night it was swaying and heaving with the weight of dead flesh and, as it crawled over the railway lines, it began to bounce and buck on its tired, tortured springs. The neatly packed bodies began to shift. A hundred, two hundred scrawny arms and legs flopped over the side, waving wildly, limply in a terrible, mocking farewell; and simultaneously from those 3,000 men, women, and children, rose a thin hopeless wail that swept from one end of the orderly queue to the other, an almost inhuman cry of despair that neither threats, nor blows, nor bullets could silence. With one last, desperate lurch, the lorry cleared the tracks, disappearing out of the arc lights, into the darkness; and then there was silence, absolute and all-embracing. For three seconds, four at the most, those French people had glimpsed the true horror of Auschwitz; but now it was gone and they could not believe what their eyes had told them. Already their minds, untrained to mass murder, had rejected the existence of the lorry; and with that they marched quietly toward the gas chambers, which claimed them half an hour later. Yet the SS realized well what could happen if mass hysteria of this nature had time to catch hold of their victims, if the lorry broke down, for instance. Every night after that, a secret signal was given when it was approaching and all arc lights were switched off until it was safely out of sight.[2]

This view from the Auschwitz ramp could not contradict the long-lived thesis among Holocaust historians that knowledge would not have helped the prospective victims in any way. Early on, Bauer came up with a solid psychological thesis about the historical events.

The information was there all the time, including information regarding the ways in which the Nazis were misleading and fooling their victims. The point is that this information was rejected, people did not want to know, because knowledge would have caused pain and suffering, and there was seemingly no way out.[3]

This version is repeated in the 1990s: "During the Holocaust countless individuals received information and rejected it, suppressed it, or rationalized about it, were thrown into despair without any possibility of acting on it"[4] and: "Information was, in other words, available about the murderous policy of the Germans. The problem was that people refused to listen, refused to believe that what they did not want to hear was the truth, refused to admit that it could happen in Hungary even if they admitted that it was happening in Poland—in short, they rejected the information."[5]

This thesis is followed by one of Professor Bauer's students: "the many details that the escapees told could not change a thing in the behavior of the Slovakian Jews."[6] This observation is also supported by Cohen: "At the end of June(!), after most Jews had been deported and gassed, an underground activist overcame his inner hesitancy, and he read the [Auschwitz] Protocols to his comrades in the labor service. They were so shocked by the revelations that they wanted to turn him in and even pounced on him for spreading horror stories."[7]

Tivadar Soros, however, did not share this view. He was among the few who were informed about the Vrba-Wetzler report, and he found the information most valuable.

My new acquaintances also enjoyed good relations with several members of the Jewish Council, or their sons, and from them they received up-to-date information. They explained to me, in confidence, that someone had succeeded in getting out of the death camp at Auschwitz and had told the whole story. There was a copy of his statement at the Council office with details of the German atrocities. We talked a lot about how we might escape.

In a phone interview George Soros confirmed that they were informed about the content of the Vrba-Wetzler report while in hiding.[8]

Can we regard Bauer's thesis as possessing strong explanatory power if the masses were not provided with any *specific* information about their impending fate? Bauer posits that even if the Hungarian Jews had believed the report, it is unlikely that it would have resulted in immediate resistance in a country that lacked hills and had no local strong resistance group and whose young men were in labor camps.[9]

Like their historians, survivors, too, are "prisoners of memory and time."[10] Vrba himself admitted that "even if, while on the ramp, we had been able to establish contact with a few of those who had just arrived . . . they would not have grasped the truth."[11] Indeed, present claims that Jews would have resisted had they been informed about Auschwitz are disputable, both historically and psychologically. Historically, because of serious external constraints, and psychologically because of the existing gap between information and knowledge, knowing and believing. Still, we do know, that when we deprive people of knowledge we a priori deprive them of power.[12] Thus, the "information" thesis remains only a "sophisticated semantic-epistemological argument."[13]

In mid-May 1944 Hungarian Jews, such as Cecila Klein, a deportee from Huszt, had no knowledge about Auschwitz.

> In mid-May we began to hear rumors of "resettlement." The very word had an encouraging ring to it. In our constant vacillating frenetic state between hope and despair, "resettlement" sounded as if we were headed for some great estate or plantation to farm or breed horses. There seemed to be no limits to the possibilities. Some even expressed the hope that we would be resettled miraculously in our own Jewish state.[14]

When she obediently arrived at the appointed meeting place, Cecila sensed right away that one of the German tactics used to rob people of knowledge was to strip them of their clothing.

First we were ordered to strip naked, men and women together. Then the women and the girls were lined up on one side and we were ordered to lie on our sides on a wooden table. While an SS officer gawked and jeered, a woman with [a] stick poked around our private parts. . . . Our very nakedness unleashed more fury and hatred from our captors. They compounded our pain and misery by hurling obscene insults at us. "Bloodsuckers, parasites who spread foul diseases. Demons doing the devil's work, whores and perverts," they called us, tormenting us as they worked themselves into frenzy. They moved rapidly from table to table, accompanied by selected citizens of Huszt, who volunteered to witness the degradation of Jewish neighbors who until recently had been their friends, even their sweethearts.[15]

Upon arrival at Auschwitz, the deportees were ready to sell all they had for knowledge, even about their impending fate.

In the eerie silence, skeletal men [of the "Canada" group] in striped pajamas moved among us like shadows, their faces a ghoulish yellow, their shaven skulls glistening with perspiration. They snatched our bags and piled them on the platform in tidy heaps. Nathan [Cecila's brother-in-law and father of a two year old] whispered a question to one of the skeletons. No answer. Nathan pushed his watch into the man's hand. . . . "Give your child to an older woman." I was close enough to hear him add, "Tonight will be the gassing and the burning of the very young and the old, the mothers with children!" Mother heard, Mina [Cecila's sister] did not. Mother approached Mina and gently taking Danny, whispered "Darling, give Danny to me. . . . I have heard that women in charge of little ones won't be sent to hard labor. You're young and you'll be able to work hard. I promise to look after Danny."[16]

Cecila and her sister Mina and brother-in-law were chosen to work. Their mother and her grandson vanished.

One may perhaps argue that no one in the Judenrat in Budapest could have been efficient enough to deliver the Auschwitz message to Cecila Klein in Huszt before her deportation; we know that travel in

Hungary was problematic.[17] Still, one may question why, a month after D-Day, Dr. Judith Magyar-Isaacson and her family were packing their luggage as if "resettlement" was something to look forward to. She recalls their ignorance regarding their imminent fate.

At 8 A.M. on July 2, 1944, we were given four hours to pack, but our rucksacks were ready. "Let's cook a decent meal," said grandmother Vago, "the beans and raspberries are perfect." Grandmother and I had tended the garden since the closing of the ghetto, and the first batch of wax beans had ripened just in time for this meal—yellow, tender, and velvety. Mother had planned to cook them "French style" with some vinegar and hoarded sugar . . . but at the last minute, grandmother Vago spooned in a small jar of her precious apricot jam. "No use saving it for the boys," she murmured. Grandmother and I were doing the dishes, when mother entered. "You forgot to sweep the hall this morning," grandmother reminded her. "Who cares?" mother retorted. "And why do you wipe those plates, Mama? Smash them to the floor, instead!" Grandmother's worn hand trembled in the mid-air, her eyes begging for pity. "Sorry, Mama," mother whispered, "I'll sweep the hall right away." And so it was that we left the place neat and clean for Mrs. Ulrich [the neighbor who wanted to take their home].[18]

The particular efforts the Germans made to maintain the deportees' level of ignorance until the last moment before the victims were gassed are worth noting. Vrba has documented them as follows.

It may seem callous, inhuman almost, that we should eat while thousands were being herded to their death. Yet there was nothing we could do to help them, for we were bound by an even more rigid rule of silence. To break it meant instant death. . . . Very occasionally, however, somebody tried, usually a newcomer who did not realize he was sacrificing his life for nothing. There was, for instance, one young Czech boy, who had been in the camp only about three months and was unloading a transport from Prague. It had been a good trip, relatively speaking, and most of the victims were in fair physical shape. One woman, in fact, was almost jaunty, bouncing along the ramp with her fur coat thrown loosely over her shoulders, and holding her two well-dressed children by the hand. The young Czech prisoner watched her, maybe with pity, maybe with nostalgia for the lush cafe society which obviously had been hers. He saw her pass an Obersturmbanhfuhrer and he heard her say to her son in a loud, almost gay voice: "Wipe your nose, dear. That's a German officer!" At that his control snapped. He edged toward her and muttered: "You stupid bitch, you'll be dead in half an hour!" She stopped and stared at him, her plump, still beautiful face sagging. Then she twirled on her heel and marched straight up to the SS man. Pointing a finger at the prisoner, she shrilled: "That . . . that convict says we're going to die. What does he mean? What is happening? What are you . . ." The SS man interrupted blandly, politely, almost apologetically. "Please, Madame," he said, "calm yourself. Nothing is going to happen to you. Kill you? Do you honestly believe we Germans are barbarians?" She turned around to face the Czech prisoner, a look of smug contempt on her face; but he was no longer there. He had been taken behind the wagons by two SS men and shot with an air pistol that made no noise and disturbed nobody, except, of course the prisoner.[19]

Langbein had the same impression about the level of information of the Auschwitz arrivals.

Of the millions of those who were murdered in Auschwitz most never saw the camp but immediately on arrival were taken to the gas chamber. The disguising of the deportation by the SS was a smoothly operating ruse. From the very first loading of the victims onto the trains for "resettlement" until they reached the gas chamber, which was disguised as showers, everything was a perfect swindle.[20]

Langbein cites the evidence of Dr. Zigmond Bender, who survived the Sonderkommando. Bender recalled that in June [actually July] 1944, when the SS transported Jews from the Lodz ghetto, the disguise was still effective. When they were brought to the crematorium, Hauptsturmfuehrer Moll (the commander of the crematorium) explained to them that they were going to this installation only for a bath and immediately after that they would be served coffee. When the new arrivals heard this, they rewarded him with applause. When some children refused to be mollified and shouted that they were thirsty now, the SS ordered that water should be brought to them at once. This ignorance of their imminent fate reached its peak when Jews were led to believe that they should make special efforts to bring wood along on their transport; it would eventually be used to burn them alive upon their arrival to Auschwitz. This document appears in the memoirs of Fiderkiewicz (1962), a doctor at Auschwitz: "Only now it became clear to us what a satanic plan the Germans had invented. A few weeks before the Hungarian Jews arrived, wagons loaded with wood reached this place."[21]

The Germans kept on investing in the deception until the last moment. At Auschwitz, a Red Cross ambulance stood ready in the middle of the railway platform.[22] In Kulka's 1986 book, *Escape from Auschwitz*, we read how two women inmates from Czechoslovakia, who like other passengers on their transport were ignorant about Auschwitz, happened to be warned by the "Canada" inmates about their impending gassing. Surprised by the strange welcome, they approached a nearby SS officer not only to complain about the information they had just received but also to ask for medical help, having noticed the ambulance. The officer offered them some pills "to calm their nerves," and asked, "Who told you such nonsense? . . . You should not believe these convicts. They try to frighten you in order to get hold of your luggage. I promise you, you will not be molested any more." The officer was the physician SS Hauptsturmfuhrer Dr. Josef Mengele. He looked for somebody who would see to it that the two women would not spread panic[23] and assigned Pestek, who was about to escape with Lederer, to this mission.

PART FOUR

Between Banality
and Politics:
Vrba and Arendt
Restaged

> The motives of memory are never pure.
> JAMES YOUNG, *The Texture of Memory*

Just before the new year of 2001, I visited the Holocaust Museum in Washington, D.C. In its exhibition, nowhere is the escape mentioned. I proceeded, as any naive viewer, to the learning center. When I asked about the Vrba-Wetzler escape and report, I received a cordial reply. The guide referred me to the English version of *Auschwitz Chronicle, 1939–1945*, the most informative chronology book on Auschwitz, where I could read a few lines on the escapees: date, number, former names, and the like.[1] "You know why they changed their names, don't you?" asked the guide. "No," I answered, and he continued, "This was done in order to protect their families." How is it that the names are missing from the exhibition but every guide knows the reason for their suppression?

Before leaving the museum, I decided to step into its book store. On central display were numerous copies of Bauer's newly published book, *Rethinking the Holocaust*.[2] I searched for Vrba's book in vain and asked the cashier. He had been working there for several years but was not familiar with the title. He was willing to check on his computer. "Yes," he said, "I found it, but the last time it appeared here was in 1994," and concluded, "They probably stopped printing it."

Interestingly, that same year, 1994, there was a conference at the United States Holocaust Museum dedicated to the fiftieth anniversary of the Hungarian Holocaust, "one of the most controversial chapters in the history of the Nazis' war against the Jews."[3] Researchers agree that the most hotly disputed part of that conference was the historiographical controversy over the role of the Hungarian Jewish Council.[4] A similar conference took place in London on April 17–18, 1994.[5] Vrba was among the participants at the Washington conference. In his presentation, Vrba posed a serious question regarding the correct representation of the event: Who is the better historian—"those of us who saw the Nazis in action in Auschwitz" or "those who did not have direct experience with the Nazis"?[6]

The following chapter questions whether we should favor the "expert discourse" over the "survivor discourse."[7]

THIRTEEN

"REAL" HISTORIANS
AND "TRUE" STORIES

In 2001, three years after Vrba's book was published in Hebrew and he himself had been awarded an honorary doctorate from the University of Haifa, a group of Slovak activists, among them Israeli Holocaust historians with ties to the Slovak community (Bauer, Yablonka, Jelinek, Fatran, and Rothkirchen) came out with a seemingly rather hastily put together volume of articles in Hebrew entitled *Leadership under Duress: The Working Group in Slovakia, 1942–1944*. The introduction explains to the Israeli readers that the volume is intended as a tribute to the Working Group. The rationale for this effort is presented as follows.

The [Slovak] Working Group has been put on the stand of the defendant by a bunch of mockers, pseudo-historians and historians, who have accused them of collaborating with the SS and concealing the truth from their own communities in Slovakia and Hungary. They claim that, had it not been for this collaboration, many could have saved themselves [the fate of] deportation to Poland. This is a false accusation for which there is no basis in facts, at least regarding the Slovak Jews, because it ignores the constraints of the Jews in Slovakia and Hungary in 1944, the topographical conditions of Hungary and the resoluteness of the local helpers to complete the work. And therefore this accusation is baseless. Regretfully, it was given legitimacy [lit. "was made kosher"] when Haifa University awarded a honorary doctorate to the head of these mockers,

Peter [*sic*] Vrba. The heroism of this person, who together with the late Alfred Wetzler, was among the first to escape from Auschwitz, is beyond doubt. But the fact that, just because he was an Auschwitz prisoner endowed with personal heroism, he has crowned himself as knowledgeable to judge all those involved in the noble work of rescue, and accuse them falsely, deeply disturbs us, the Czech community.

As to their credentials, the participants of the volume conclude their introduction as follows, "We, Czechoslovakian descendants, who personally experienced [the war], cannot remain silent in face of these false accusations. With all its horrors, this history is a narrative: We are not just telling history, we tell memories and first-hand experiences. These are our own memories and experiences. Our position in this regard is very clear."[1]

In his own 2001 book, *Rethinking the Holocaust*, Bauer argues that the "real historian," is "a person who tells (true) stories." He is a person who is engaged in "post facto reconstruction of the course of human events in accordance with certain rules of sifting facts and analyzing sources."[2] Bauer further suggests that historians are not supposed to ask "what if" questions, yet he is quick to acknowledge that most of them, "in fact do so."[3] Following this line of inquiry we are obliged to ask: What if the Hungarian Jews had read the Vrba-Wetzler report and believed it? What if Israeli high school students had been given a chance to read Vrba's memoirs and draw their own conclusions?

It was to such questions that Mr. Ben Ami, the book's translator, hoped to get an answer. The response he received from Bauer in Hebrew was the following:

Dear Mr. Ben Ami,

Thank you for sending me Vrba's book and the correspondence pertaining to it. I am, of course, familiar with the book. In itself this is an important document and Rudolf Vrba, in my eyes, is one of the Jewish Heroes of the Holocaust. Therefore, I made efforts—but failed—to convince the Hebrew University to award him an honorary doctorate;

however, I made further efforts at the University of Haifa and there I succeeded. The book, in fact, is not a memoir in the usual sense. It contains excerpts of conversations of which there is no chance that they are accurate and it has elements of a second-hand story that does not necessarily correspond with reality. Everything he tells about himself and about his actions, on the contrary, is not only the truth, but also [forms] a document of significant historical value. I truly regret that Yad Vashem did not publish the book in Hebrew. On the other hand, Vrba's wild attacks on Kasztner and on the Slovak underground are all a-historical and simply wrong from the start, and in that respect I am glad [the book] does not carry the name of Yad Vashem. You have probably gathered by now that I am split in my attitude. I have set out this attitude in my article in the German journal after Vrba, who knows me personally, attacked me and my ideas. I admired Vrba, with true admiration—though mixed with resistance to his thoughts in historical matters in which he thinks he is an expert, though I am not sure that he is justified in thinking so.

Yours,
Yehuda Bauer

The publication in 1998 of Vrba's book in Hebrew enabled scholars from different disciplines to finally challenge the "expert discourse" and stop relating to Vrba's memoirs as a "reserved text" reflecting the voice of stigmatized individuals and groups rather than an "integrative text."[4] This tendency comes to the fore in Michal Shaked's 2001 article on the representation of the Kasztner trial in the Israeli national memory. Shaked questions the "experts discourse" during the Kasztner's trial and wonders why it labeled the Vrba-Wetzler report as "notes from Auschwitz" ("Yediot Auschwitz" in Hebrew).[5] She reiterates that Bauer's thesis represents the hegemonic narrative as voiced by Judge Agranat at that trial: the belief that revealing the information of the Vrba-Wetzler report would have been of no use, dismissing the possibility that informed Diaspora Jews might have been transformed from sheep going to the slaughter into resisting sheep. She describes Vrba as a rare Jewish hero and refers the reader to his memoirs in Hebrew. But Shaked is not an Israeli historian. She is an Israeli lawyer.

Paradoxically, Vrba's voice was first given academic legitimacy not by the Israelis but rather by the Germans. In 1996, he was invited to present his version of the story by a most prestigious journal, *Viertel-jahrshefte fuer Zeitgeschichte*, which tried to facilitate a dialogue between the Auschwitz escapee and the Israeli Holocaust historians.

Bauer's 1997 response in this journal appears also in its Hebrew version in the 2001 joint volume of these historians. In his article Bauer agrees with Vrba that the Hungarian Jews who were deported to Auschwitz were ignorant of their impending fate. Yet, as before, he adduces strong reasons for their powerlessness and their inability to resist. He restates the thesis, familiar in his writings since 1978, that in Hungary (and probably elsewhere) the Jews could not translate their information into knowledge, so that the question of information becomes almost irrelevant as most of the informed denied the information.

Bauer agrees that there was an interval of one or two weeks at the most between the arrival of the report in Hungary and the start of the massive deportations during mid-May 1944. Claiming to see the large picture, Bauer gives this gap in the chronology less weight than Vrba. But it is here that we can take our cue from Walter Benjamin and examine this "gap" as a porous surface whose holes provide windows into discarded memories.[6] It is the location where Bauer's expert discourse and Vrba's "survivor discourse" collide.

Although Bauer agrees with Vrba's criticism of the ineffectiveness of the Hungarian Judenrat, this does not imply collaboration. And after all, there were a variety of Judenrate, some of whom saw individual bravery as disobedience and delaying the German's demands for possessions or lives as some form of success.

Bauer sees the delay in the dissemination of the report as a technical issue: "It was proven that the content of the report was known in Budapest." Elsewhere he admits that until the escape, there were only rumors about this center of death. If Vrba sees things differently, it is because he is a "bitter victim" who unrealistically expected too much of his initiative. Vrba is also an "inaccurate" historian as he states that the Kasztner train carried 1,800 passengers, while in fact the right number is 1,684. Incidentally, Bauer himself gives the number as 1,700 in his book *Jews for Sale?*[7] Vrba is further chastised for his ignorance of Hebrew:[8] Had Vrba known that language he could have read more documents from the Holocaust in Hebrew and learned the "truth." Vrba believes that survivors' understanding is superior to those who had no direct experience of the Nazis: "For those of us who saw the Nazis in action in Auschwitz" the following basic tenet is easier to understand. "If the Nazis entered into any 'negotiations' with Jewish Councils in Bratislava or Budapest, it was to use the latter for their own objectives: to rob Jews swiftly of their personal property, to prepare lists of those to be deported on the basis of names and addresses supplied by the Jewish Councils, to make those on the lists board the deportation trains without causing difficulties, and to kill the deportees economically and efficiently once in Auschwitz, all the while preserving the secret of their murderous empire."[9] In the expert discourse, the fact that the prominent passengers in Kasztner's train knew about Auschwitz is proof that the information was disseminated. In the "survivor discourse," the fact that the specifically informed acted on that information meant that they had been able to grasp its implications without denial.

This tension between expert discourse and survivor discourse revealed in the 1997 dialogue remains present in Bauer's *Rethinking the Holocaust*. In it, Bauer admits that "the protocols were an important factor in stopping the deportations,"[10] a linear conclusion yet to make it into Hebrew high school text books on the Holocaust. Even within this conciliatory atmosphere Bauer cannot explain how it happened that for so many years he had documented the "unqualified heroism" of Vrba and Wetzler anonymously, calling them "young Slovak Jews," without citing Vrba's memoirs, and treating the escape in a reserved manner. Bauer's *Rethinking the Holocaust* contains no new information or an explanation as to how Dr. Neumann, the report's architect, could have forgotten to include the warning of the "Hungarian salami" in the text. At the same time, he tells his readers in a small note that the alarming message is missing in the Vrba-Wetzler report thereby again clouding the issue as he leaves the reader with the impression that there is something wrong with Vrba's credibility.[11] In the course of his 2001, ten-page account of the escape from Auschwitz, the report, and its dissemination, Bauer variously described Vrba as "[a] bitter Auschwitz survivor," "not credible," "embittered and furious," and "[his] despair and bitterness are overdone."[12]

Bauer believes that wartime Jewish leaders who saved Jews ought to be remembered, Rumkowski included, despite his general abuse of power as well. After all, argues Bauer, Rumkowski "did have a point." History shows that there was a higher percentage of survivors from the Lodz ghetto "than from most other places because, thanks in part to Rumkowski's draconian policies, the Lodz ghetto was the last one in Eastern Europe to be liquidated."[13] Thus, Kasztner was right because of his good intentions. Rumkowski was right because of the consequences of his actions. Vrba was not.

Vested with a legitimacy imparted by expertise, some historians, nevertheless, often express the belief that redemptive closure is both possible and desirable. Echoing Yad Vashem's "expert discourse," Cesarani writes: "After the war survivors suspected that the [so-called] 'Kasztner train' was at best a one-off opportunity that the Zionists had engineered to save their own skins or, at worst, a kind of down payment on their complicity in the deportations. In return for the trainload it was alleged that they declined to warn Jews in the provinces, allowing them to be rounded up and deported with the minimum of resistance. This calumny can now be finally laid to rest."[14] But can it be laid to rest as equally for the informed as for the uninformed? Vrba is not sure. It seems that it is exactly here, at the juncture of the expert and survivor discourses that historicization reaches it limits. At the individual level, or in the survivor discourse, argues Friedlander, "a redemptive closure (conforming or healing in effect), desirable as it would be, seems largely impossible."[15]

Bauer's position in *Rethinking the Holocaust* (2001) raises the serious question of whether a redemptive closure is ever possible. According to LaCapra, the historian ought to develop "an exchange with the 'other' that is both sensitive to transferential displacement and open to the challenge of the other's voice."[16] But did it really happen in this case?

In 2001, Bauer's criticism of Vrba is further echoed in the criticism he levels at Daniel Goldhagen. Both are charged with limited under-standing of history as they are not historians and ignorant of Hebrew. Consequently, it is questionable for Bauer that they could ever be good Holocaust interpreters. Bauer believes that Goldhagen is correct to em-phasize the personal, physical confrontation between the actual mur-derers and their Jewish victims in the ghettos, labor camps, and death marches because not enough has been said about it—"apart from Israeli historians whom Goldhagen cannot read because of the language barrier and apart from a deluge of memoirs in English, which he can read and use but does not."[17] But is there really a specific language for Holocaust research other than German?[18]

Bauer believes that Goldhagen is right when he points to the central role of ideology but does not share his explanation of the phenomenon. In some places, Goldhagen ideas are far from being original: "In Israel, Yisrael Gutman, Otto Dov Kulka, and myself, among others, have been arguing for a position not dissimilar, in this respect, from Goldhagen's own. . . . For Goldhagen to say that he was the first to have discovered that a specific German way led to the Holocaust, a way shaped by rad-ical anti-semitism, is not credible."[19]

The only staging that awaited Goldhagen in Israel was a lecture in a room closed to the wider public. But, unlike Vrba, the commercial suc-cess of his book guaranteed that his voice did become heard and cre-ated public discussion, also among Hebrew readers. Bauer is rather amazed by the success Goldhagen achieved as the book of this young "Harvard tutor" contains little or no evidence he "knows [any] lan-guages other than English and German."[20]

After contributing to a 1997 joint volume that aimed to refute Gold-hagen's work,[21] Bauer confesses in 2001: "I have consciously moder-ated my criticism, largely because of the violent attacks on the young Harvard scholar. In Israel, I defended him publicly against vicious per-sonal attacks and invited him to a *closed* discussion at Yad Vashem with Israeli scholars who held various views on his work."[22]

We are not informed whether Vrba's book, too, has been previously dis-cussed in closed rooms in Yad Vashem. We know, however, that it did not become a commercial success, although it was available in English, French, German, Dutch, and Czech before finally being published in Hebrew. Yet, the fear of success is there for Vrba as well. Otherwise, how could one explain the friendly warning that I received from a respected historian: "I have the feeling that you have been seduced by Vrba's contention"?[23]

Bauer believes that Goldhagen "had unfortunately failed to show that humility that a researcher should when approaching the Holocaust."[24] He sees him as "[a]n American Jew who took the place of the father confessor, a real life Harvard professor who dressed his message like an academic exercise so beloved of many Westerners, including Germans, [which] made the whole experience even more satisfying. Again, it was the simplistic nature of the message that made it so palatable."[25]

Thus Goldhagen, the "young Harvard scholar" and Vrba, the "young Slovak Jew," are both wrong. Goldhagen is chided for failing to show humility in approaching the Holocaust. As for Vrba, his testimony is credible, but his interpretation is problematic.[26] Yet, both Goldhagen's and Vrba's appeal to the wider public remain a mystery. Some personality variables seem to be at stake: Vrba is wrong but seductive; Goldhagen is wrong but is a "gifted scholar." Unlike Goldhagen, Vrba is not ignorant of languages but knows about nine (Czech, English, Slovak, Hungarian, German, Russian, French, Latin, and Yiddish). He is not the son of a survivor (like Goldhagen) but a survivor himself. Like Goldhagen, he cannot be dismissed easily—he is the only escapee who is an academic, trained in the exact sciences, and knows what objectivity is all about.

What should one do in such cases? Bauer promised "that the controversy [between him and Goldhagen] would be civilized." Though Bauer can assure himself and us that Goldhagen with his book will not make it into the pantheon of Holocaust scholars, "his faulty thesis provoked a discussion about essentials, and for that at least he should be thanked." He concludes by reiterating that he has moderated his criticism of Goldhagen over the years and has come round to defending him publicly.

Bauer believes that academic discussion should be honest and open, and criticism, even sharp criticism, should be voiced. And he adds, "but I am opposed to witch-hunting."[27]

FOURTEEN

NAKED VICTIMS, DRESSED-UP MEMORIES

I was barely 16 years old when I arrived at Auschwitz from Hungary . . . shy and reserved. . . . Mengele was there and everything was so organized and went so well. . . . We were ordered to undress and take a disinfecting shower. . . . a piece of rag was quickly thrown to each of the girls but when my turn came there was no more clothing. . . . I was naked for four weeks. . . . the SS officers would come to watch me every morning and afternoon during the roll calls. . . . I cannot talk about it even today. . . . we never heard about Auschwitz while in Hungary.

AN AUSCHWITZ SURVIVOR, VANCOUVER, CANADA, APRIL 4, 2000

Acknowledging that the principle of knowing or interpreting the past is embedded in the present,[1] we are required to question again, with LaCapra, "What aspects of the past should be remembered and how should they be remembered? Are there phenomena whose traumatic nature blocks understanding and disrupts memory while producing belated effects that have an impact on attempts to represent or otherwise address the past? . . . Can—or should—historiography define itself in a purely scholarly and professional way that distances it from public memory and its ethical implications?"[2] Should Horthy be remembered as a leader who contributed (albeit unwillingly) to the smoothness and speed of the deportation of the 437,000 Hungarian Jews from the countryside or as a leader who took measures to oppose the deportation of the 200,000 remaining Budapest Jews?[3] Should the members of the Slovak or the Hungarian Judenrat be remembered as Nazi-approved compliant leaders or as brave men who tried to save the remaining Jews? Should the escapees from Auschwitz be remembered as individuals who added glory to the narrative of Jewish resistance by their consistent opposition to the plans of the Nazis or as individuals who refused to comply with the hegemonic Israeli Holocaust narrative, where those who criticize the wartime Jewish leadership are allotted a purely anonymous role? Should the leaders of the Working Group (whether Gizi Fleishmann, Oskar Neumann, or Rabbi Weissmandel) be remembered as collaborators or rescuers if they negotiated with the SS without spelling out what knowledge they would provide and what knowledge they would conceal?[4] Should Hannah Arendt be remembered as a Jewish woman living in a Manhattan apartment who became detached from her Jewish heritage or as a German-American Jewish scholar who did not fear to question the dark parts of the unmastered past?[5]

The silencing of Vrba's voice and of the morally frightening past that it represents could be dealt with by purges, by forgetting, by trials, or by pedagogy ("history lessons").[6] To this one may add the position of moral naiveté. Fatran, for example, calls for our sympathetic acknowledgment of the following: "On the night of September 26 [1944] the U.Z. offices were broken into and a *card index* containing a list *with details of the remaining Jews* was stolen. When the activists reported this to [Alois] Brunner, he frowned *sympathetically and promised an investigation and punishment for those responsible.*"[7] Fatran does not elaborate on this call for empathy. While the members of the Working Group, when they "called on him for help," might have been unaware of the atrocities Brunner, Eichmann's most evil henchman, had committed at Drancy, the average reader of Fatran can be expected to know this by now. Can she explain this sanctimonious way of writing with the same naiveté in 1994? Can the Working Group be regarded as an underground organization if their lives depended on the deportation list of their community?

George Klein's account suggests that the distinction between information and knowledge proved right and wrong at the same time. It proved right because Klein, indeed, did not believe the information: "I read the [Vrba-Wetzler] report a few weeks after it was prepared. It was one of the first copies prepared from the original that Kasztner and the other members of the Jewish Council had received. My supervisor gave me permission to tell my relatives and close friends about the report so that they could go underground in time. Of a dozen or so people I warned, not one believed me." But it was found also wrong—Klein reveals that his strength to resist came from being an *informed Jew:* "It was relatively easy for me to believe [the] report. I was young and vigorous and had nothing to lose. Nevertheless, I hesitated until the very last moment. It was not until I saw the freight cars in front of me that I had the courage to run, despite the risk of being shot."[8]

Forty years after this informed Jewish youth succeeded in escaping the final solution, he happened to see the Lanzmann documentary one evening and thus encountered the informer, Vrba: "I suddenly realized this is the man who saved my life," he told me during his visit to Jerusalem in 2002. "I immediately took the first plane to Vancouver in order to meet this man and shake his hand." Klein and Vrba became friends who admire each other for what each of them achieved in his life. But somehow, or maybe naturally, the escapee—the informer—and the saved—the informed—do not equally share the thesis of "knowing" and "not believing." Vrba does not stop questioning the establishment's intentions, be it the Jewish leaders, the leading historians, or even me, the Israeli Sabra researcher who had assumed he would want to cooperate with me right away. Klein is not as confident that the establishment is to be blamed. Having seen how his close relatives whom he had informed about the report still boarded the trains, he considers Bauer's thesis as the most representative of the situation.

The immediate regaining of courage among the uninformed in the face of knowledge was also observed by Langbein, one of the leaders of the underground resistance in Auschwitz, who writes: "Little is known about the resistance attempts of those who were immediately selected . . . for the gas chamber. It will never be known how many desperate acts occurred before the poison gas took effect. Only a few have been documented. On May 25, 1944, a few hundred Hungarian Jews attempted to hide in the ditches and undergrowth around the gas chambers. The SS hunted them down with flashlights and shot them. Three days later, a similar escape was attempted with the same results."[9] If the Hungarians had the power and courage to resist while naked in Auschwitz, how strong might they have been when still clothed in Hungary?

Within this context, the dialogue between Vrba and Bauer about the thesis of "knowing" and "not believing" may serve as a most intriguing form of academic staging. Both are German speakers, and their dialogue took place in one of the most prestigious historical journals in Germany. It is intriguing, not necessarily as part of the pursuit of historical truth, but for questioning the ways in which seeking the truth has itself become the subject of inquiry.[10]

On German soil, the voice of the history maker and the history interpreter were clearly understood: Fifty years after the war, the German audience was most sensitive to stories that had not been told or were not being told, or had been accidentally forgotten.[11] The contrasts were evident in this meeting between two academics from two different ideological and scientific cultures: Dr. Bauer, the disengaged historian from the school of Yosef Talmon, who claims to be objective in his search for facts as an outside observer, and Dr. Vrba, the biochemist, whose subjective and engaging memory holds a remarkable number of figures and who does not hide his subjectivity as a participant observer in the Holocaust. It is a meeting between an Israeli, a previously left-leaning kibbutz member, the son of Czechoslovak Zionist Jewish leaders who were lucky to obtain a last-minute certificate for Palestine in 1938; and a former Holocaust victim whose parents did not want to or could not hear the warning of the Zionists to leave the Diaspora in time. It is a dialogue between an Israeli who views Israel as the sole solution for the safety of the Jews and the non-Israeli Jew who refuses to view the Zionist entity as his major concern, who actually still fears the thought that again he might be "saved" by leaders! It is a dialogue between the expert discourse and the survivor discourse, between the Zionist self and the Diaspora other.[12] And "the 'other' can only be known and made present in that to which it is opposed and from which it has to remain forever separated."[13] It is also a dialogue between an Israeli scholar who wants to believe that the Zionist underground was a priori a just organization and a Canadian scholar and former Auschwitz prisoner, whose experience taught him that any anti-Nazi resistance organization, whether composed of Jews, Poles, or Communists, had moral limitations, given its preferential care for its own members.

The publication in Hebrew of Vrba's writings and memoirs has opened new doors to Hebrew-reading Israelis. It seems to replace the indisputable thesis of knowing and not believing with questions about the distinction between knowing a general piece of information and a specific one, between knowing the leaders and believing them. It further raises questions about the historians' awareness of the facts and the willingness to confront the facts: facts that were sometimes "too much to take."[14]

The Bauer–Vrba dialogue, more than fifty years after Auschwitz, illustrates the power of discourse. It shows how the present-day conceptions of the past are constructed by that power—the power to decide what is to be forgotten, dismissed, suppressed, disregarded, discredited, and left nameless and the power to define who is the martyr, who the hero, and who the author of memory, as the full name of Yad Vashem—The Holocaust Martyrs' and Heroes' Remembrance Authority—clearly spells out. It is a dialogue between the known and the "could-be-known."[15] It may even be a crossroads at which Jerusalem, Manhattan, and Auschwitz can somehow meet.[16]

A year after his dialogue with Vrba, Bauer chose to take on board some of Vrba's carefully observed facts. He now seems to agree with him that under the Nazis' satanic terror, even beloved and brave Jewish Zionist leaders who wished to rescue Jews were transformed into moral hostages.

Because the Working Group, under Fleischmann's leadership, believed that their tactic had worked during the previous regime, they tried to ap-

NAKED VICTIMS, DRESSED-UP MEMORIES · **123**

ply the same tactic to the new circumstances. They went to the Nazis and offered them goods in return for a cessation of the deportations of Jews, despite warnings from some friendly SS contacts not to enter negotiations with SS officer Alois Brunner. When they were told to ask the Jews of Bratislava to report for deportation to Sered, they obeyed. When their community list was taken by the [local Slovak] police, they complained to the SS *but did not spread the word to the community to hide.* . . . The month of September [1944], the last period of the Working Group activity, casts a dark shadow over all of them, and on Gizi as their leader. They could have no illusions by then, but *they acted just like many of the Jewish Councils in Poland.* They could have warned the Jews, but they didn't; they could have refused the demands of the Nazis—even though this would have made no difference—but they didn't. But then, we were not in their place, and we don't know how we would have acted.[17]

An e-mail message received by Vrba on Tuesday, October 2, 2001 at 00:08:52

Dear Prof. Vrba,

I will start by saying that your book is by far the book that has left the strongest impact on me. I will never forget it. Other than the change it brought upon me regarding the way I see the history of my people, I have a far more cynical attitude to the 'state-sponsored' approach (still prevailing in Israel) to the Holocaust.

I am 27 years old, a software engineer from Israel. I have read a lot of books relating to European history from the demise of Napoleon onward. I must say that I had had a tendency to avoid the subject of the Holocaust. I could not bring myself to read about horrors that were beyond my ability to comprehend. Your book is unique in the sense (one amongst many. It is also a literary masterpiece!) that it focused on the way of deception that enabled the Nazis to lead millions of Jews, with little resistance, to the gas chambers, rather than on the horrors themselves (like most books in Israel do). I think that your coverage of 'the economics of the Holocaust' (so to say), enabled me to try to understand not only how this mass-murder could be achieved, but also why. I read the book originally in Hebrew. I then recommended the book to a good Slovak friend of mine (actually from Topolocany, your town), who eventually bought the book in its English edition. We have both agreed if one has to read one, and only one, book relating to the holocaust, then yours is definitely the one. It should be read by every school boy in Israel, but I venture to believe that the educational authorities there will not let this happen. Your book will not be in line with the Zionist clichés.

I could have lingered writing about my very strong impact from your book, but I reckon that you are a very busy person (I understood that scientific research work takes majority of your time). I will apologize that language limitations (English is not my native tongue) made this letter cumbersome. I wanted to write it some time ago.

I wish you health and many years of active life! I hope you will continue bravely bringing your message to those who are interested in the truth.

(Name and address known to the author)

ACKNOWLEDGMENTS

1. Arendt, H. "Truth and Politics," in *Philosophy, Politics and Society*, eds. P. Laslett and W.G. Runciman (Oxford: Blackwell, 1967), 113.
2. Vrba, R. "Footnote to the Auschwitz Report," *Jewish Currents* 20, no. 3 (1966): 22–28; Vrba, R. and R. Manwell. "The Camps: An Inside View," in *History of the Second World War*, vol. 5, ed. B. L. Hart (London: Purnell and Sons, 1968), 2148–2156; Vrba, R. "Die missachtete Warnung. Betrachtungen ueber den Auschwitz-Bericht 1944." *Vierteljahrshefte fuer Zeitgeschichte* 44, Heft 1 (1996): 1–24; Vrba, R. "Vergebliche Warnung, Bericht ueber eine Flucht aus Auschwitz," in *Die Erfahrung des Exils. Exemplarische Reflexionen*, eds. W. Benz and M. Neiss (Berlin: Metropol, 1997), 104–124; Vrba, R. "The Preparations for the Holocaust in Hungary: An Eyewitness Account," in *The Holocaust in Hungary: Fifty Years Later*, eds. R. L. Braham and A. Pok (New York: Columbia University Press, 1997), 227–284; Vrba, R. "The Preparations for the Holocaust in Hungary: An Eyewitness Account," in *The Nazis' Last Victims: The Holocaust in Hungary*, eds. R. L. Braham and S. Miller (Detroit: Wayne State University Press, 1998), 55–102; Vrba, R. and A. Bestic. *I Cannot Forgive* (London: Sidgwick & Jackson Ltd., 1963); Vrba, R. and A. Bestic. *Escape from Auschwitz* (New York: Grove Press, 1964). Other editions in 1985, 1989, Canada 1997. A significantly expanded edition was published in 2002 under the title *I Escaped from Auschwitz* (Fort Lee, N.J., USA: Barricade Books). During the past forty years (1963–2003), numerous paperback editions of this book (sometimes with a modified title) appeared in English (London: Corgi, 1964; New York: Bantam Books, 1964; New York: Black Cat Edition, 1985; Bellingham, USA: Starr and Cross, 1989; and Vancouver, Canada: Regent College Publishing, 1997). Also translations of the book appeared in German (Munich: Ruetten and Loening, 1964, and Munich: Piper, 1997); French (Paris: Ramsay, 1988, 2001, and Paris: Presses Pocket, 1989); Dutch (Kampen: Kok Voorhoeve, 1996); Czech (Prague: Sefer, 1998); and Hebrew (Tel-Aviv: Zmora

Bitan, 1998). Thus, these memoirs appeared over forty years in numerous editions, in six languages, and became a classic of its genre.

INTRODUCTION

1. See the following works: Bauer, Y. *Jews for Sale? Nazi-Jewish Negotiations, 1933–1945* (New Haven: Yale University Press, 1994); Braham, R. L. *The Politics of Genocide: The Holocaust in Hungary* (Detroit: Wayne State University Press, 2000); Gilbert, M. *Auschwitz and the Allies* (New York: Holt Rinehart and Winston, 1981); Hilberg, R. *Perpetrators, Victims, Bystanders: The Jewish Catastrophe, 1933–1945* (New York: Aaron Asher Books, 1992); Levai, J. *Zsidosors europaban* (Budapest: Magyar Teka, 1948); Swiebocki, H., ed. *London Has Been Informed: Reports by Auschwitz Escapees* (Oswiecim: Auschwitz-Birkenau State Museum, 1997); Vrba and Manwell, "Camps: An Inside View," 2138–2158; Wyman, D. S. *The Abandonment of the Jews: America and the Holocaust, 1941–1945* (New York: Pantheon Books, 1984).

See also: Conway, J. S. "Fruhe Augenzeugenberichte aus Auschwitz, Glaubwurdigkeit und Wirkungsgeschichte." *Vierteljahrshefte fur Zeitgeschichte* 27 (1979): 260–284; Conway, J. S. "The First Report about Auschwitz." *Simon Wiesenthal Center Annual* 1 (1984): 133–151; Conway, J. S. "Der Holocaust in Ungarn." *Vierteljahrshefte fur Zeitgeschichte* 32 (1984): 179–212; Conway, J. S. "The Holocaust in Hungary: Recent Controversies and Reconsiderations," in *The Tragedy of Hungarian Jewry: Essays, Documents, Depositions,* ed. R. L. Braham (New York: Columbia University Press, 1986), 1–48; Kulka, E. "Five Escapes from Auschwitz," in *They Fought Back,* ed. Y. Shul (New York: Schocken Books, 1968/1975), 212–237; Kulka, E. "The Escape of Jewish Prisoners and Their Attempts to Stop the Annihilation," in *The Nazi Concentration Camps: Lectures and Discussions,* eds. I. Gutman and A. Saf (Jerusalem: Yad Vashem, 1984) (Hebrew).

2. Braham, R. *The Politics of Genocide: The Holocaust in Hungary* (New York: Columbia University Press, 1981); Neumann, O. *Im Schatten des Todes; ein Tatsachenbericht vom Schicksalskampf des slovakischen Judentums* (Tel-Aviv: Edition 'Olamenu,' 1956).

3. Braham, R. L. and S. Miller. *The Nazis' Last Victims: The Holocaust in Hungary* (Detroit: Wayne State University Press, 1998); Bauer, Y. "Conclusion: The Holocaust in Hungary—Was rescue possible?" in *Genocide and Rescue: The Holocaust in Hungary 1944,* ed. D. Cesarani (Oxford; New York: Berg,

1997), 193–209; Bauer, Y. "Anmerkungen zum 'Auschwitz-Bericht' von Rudolf Vrba." *Vierteljahrshefte fur Zeitgeschichte* 45 (1997): 297–307.
4. Lipstadt, D. E. *Beyond Belief: The American Press and the Coming of the Holocaust, 1933–1945* (New York: Free Press, 1986).
5. Bauer, *Jews for Sale?*; Bauer, Y. "Anmerkungen zum 'Auschwitz-Bericht' von Rudolf Vrba," 297–307; Gutman, I. and R. Rozett, eds. *Encyclopedia of the Holocaust* (New York: Macmillan, 1990).
6. Bauer, Y. *Rethinking the Holocaust* (New Haven, Conn.: Yale University Press, 2001); Braham and Pok, *Holocaust in Hungary.*
7. Fiderkiewicz, A. *Brzezinka, Birkenau* (Warsaw: Czytelnik, 1962); Isaacson, J. M. *Seed of Sarah: Memoirs of a Survivor* (Chicago: University of Illinois Press, 1991); Kertesz, I. *Roman Eines Schicksalslosen* (Berlin: Rowohlt Taschenbuch Verlag, 1996); Langbein, H. *Menschen in Auschwitz* (Vienna: Europaverl, 1972); Langbein, H. *Against All Hope: Resistance in the Nazi Concentration Camps, 1938–1945* (New York: Paragon House, 1994).
8. Quoted in Nicholls, W. *Christian Anti-Semitism: A History of Hate* (Northvale, N.J.: J. Aronson, 1993), 353.
9. Braham, *Politics of Genocide.*
10. Linn, R. *What Do Our Students Know about Holocaust Heroes?* (Unpublished paper, University of Haifa, Israel, 1998).
11. Ibid.
12. Bartov, O. *Murder in Our Midst: The Holocaust, Industrial Killing, and Representation* (New York: Oxford University Press, 1996); Cole, T. *Selling the Holocaust: From Auschwitz to Schindler: How History is Bought, Packaged, and Sold* (New York: Routledge, 1999).
13. Hochhuth, R. *The Deputy* (Jerusalem: Shoken, 1964) (Translation to Hebrew).
14. Gutman, I., C. Schatzker, Y. Mais, and I. Sivan. *The Holocaust and Its Significance* (Jerusalem: Zalman Shazar Center, Historical Society of Israel, 1984).
15. Bauer, Y. *The Holocaust in Historical Perspective* (Seattle: University of Washington Press, 1982); Bauer, Y. and N. Keren. *A History of the Holocaust* (New York: F. Watts, 1982); Keren, N. *Sho'ah: masa el ha-zikaron* (Tel Aviv: Sifre Tel Aviv, 1999) (Hebrew).
16. See Lanzmann, C. *Shoah: An Oral History of the Holocaust—The Complete Text of the Film* (New York: Pantheon Books, 1985).
17. The phrase comes from Handelman, D. and L. Shamgar-Handelman. "The Presence of the Absence: The Memorialism of National Death in Israel,"

in *Grasping Land: Space and Place in Contemporary Israeli Discourse and Experience*, eds. E. Ben Ari and Y. Bilu (Albany: State University of New York Press, 1997).

18. Vrba and Bestic, *I Cannot Forgive;* Vrba and Bestic, *Escape from Auschwitz.*

19. See also Ben Ami, Y. *Hashtika: Madua lo pursam hameida al Auschwitz bamoed?* (Tel-Aviv: Private publication, 1994) (Hebrew). Joffroy, P. "A Spy for God: The Ordeal of Kurt Gerstein." *The Gerstein Report* (London: Collin St. James, 1971).

20. Arendt, H. *Eichmann in Jerusalem: A Report on the Banality of Evil* (New York: Penguin, 1963).

21. Novick, P. *The Holocaust in American Life* (Boston: Houghton Mifflin, 1999), 134.

22. *Yediot Acharonot,* June 2, 1998. For more details, see Linn, R., "The Escape from Auschwitz: Why Weren't We Told about It in School?" *Theory and Criticism* 24 (2004) (Hebrew).

23. Walzer, M. *The Company of Critics: Social Criticism and Political Commitment in the Twentieth Century* (New York: Basic Books, 1988), 148.

24. *Ha'aretz,* August 19, 1998.

25. Wyschnogrod, E. *An Ethics of Remembering: History, Heterology, and the Nameless Others* (Chicago: University of Chicago Press, 1998).

PART ONE   BETWEEN AUSCHWITZ AND MANHATTAN

1. Ring, J. *The Political Consequences of Thinking: Gender and Judaism in the Work of Hannah Arendt* (Albany: State University of New York Press, 1997).

2. Browning, C. R. *Ordinary Men: Reserve Police Battalion 101 and the Final Solution in Poland* (New York: Aaron Asher Books, 1992); Browning, C. R. "Ordinary Germans or Ordinary Men? A Reply to the Critics," in *The Holocaust and History: The Known, the Unknown, the Disputed, and the Reexamined,* eds. M. Berenbaum and A. J. Peck (Bloomington: Indiana University Press, 1998).

3. Goldhagen, D. J. *Hitler's Willing Executioners: Ordinary Germans and the Holocaust* (London: Little, Brown, 1996).

4. Milgram, S. *Obedience to Authority: An Experimental View* (New York: Harper & Row, 1974); Staub, E. *The Roots of Evil: The Origins of Genocide and Other Group Violence* (New York: Cambridge University Press, 1989).

5. Hilberg, R. *The Destruction of the European Jews* (Chicago: Quadrangle Books, 1961).

6. Trunk, I. *Judenrat: The Jewish Councils in Eastern Europe under Nazi Occupation* (New York: Macmillan, 1972); Tushnet, L. *The Pavement of Hell* (New York: St. Martin's Press, 1972).

7. Ring, *Political Consequences of Thinking.*

8. Arendt, *Eichmann in Jerusalem.*

9. *Observer,* September 15, 1963; emphasis added.

10. Arendt, *Eichmann in Jerusalem.*

11. Hecht, B. *Perfidy.* (New York: Messner, 1961).

12. Yablonka, H. "Preparing the Eichmann Trial: Who Really Did the Job?" *Theoretical Inquiries in Law* 1, no. 2 (2000): 369–392 (p. 379); Yablonka, H. *The State of Israel vs Adolf Eichmann* (Tel Aviv: Yediot Acharonot, 2001), 179.

13. Friedlander, S. *Nazi Germany and the Jews* (New York: Harper and Collins, 1997).

ONE THE INFORMANTS

1. Braham, *Politics of Genocide* (2000); Gilbert, *Auschwitz and the Allies.*

2. Kulka, "Five Escapes from Auschwitz"; Kulka, "Escape of Jewish prisoners."

3. Kulka, E. *Escape from Auschwitz.* (Mass.: Bergin and Garvey Publishers, 1986).

4. Langbein, *Against All Hope.*

5. Barkai, A. *Leo Baeck: Leadership and Thought 1933–1945.* (Jerusalem: The Zalman Shazar Center for Jewish History and Leo Baeck Institute, 2000), 69, 72. See also Gutman and Rozett, *Encyclopedia of the Holocaust,* 145. Involved, against his will, with constructing lists of deportees from Theresienstadt since 1941, Baeck also maintained the philosophy that it was better that Jewish officers would "help assemble the Jews in preparation for their deportations . . . because they would be more gentle than the Gestapo. . . . [and] it was not within . . . [the Judenrat's] power to resist this command effectively." Many agree that Baeck's "mistakes in his judgments . . . ought to be included in any historiographical piece." This, however, does not prevent the authorities from widely commemorating his life's work in Israel and in the world.

6. Kulka, *Escape from Auschwitz.*

7. Braham, *Politics of Genocide,* 709.

8. Spitzer, J. *I Did Not Want to be a Jew.* (Pittsburgh: Dorrance Publishing, 1997).

9. Vrba, "Preparations for the Holocaust in Hungary" (1997), 240–241.

10. Vrba and Bestic, *Escape from Auschwitz,* 252.

11. Ibid., 217.

12. Ibid., 256.

13. See Baron, F. "The Myth and Reality of Rescue from the Holocaust: The Karski-Koestler and Vrba-Wetzler Reports," in *German-speaking Exiles in Great Britain,* ed. I. Wallace. Volume 2 of The Yearbook of the Research Center for German and Austrian Exiles Duties (Amsterdam: Rodopi, 2000), 171–208; Gilbert, *Auschwitz and the Allies.*

14. Ironically, according to Kulka, who was a prisoner in Birkenau, "The conditions for an escape from Birkenau was easier in comparison to the other Auschwitz camps," 314.

15. Vrba, "Preparations for the Holocaust in Hungary," 55–101.

16. Gilbert, *Auschwitz and the Allies.*

17. Tchuy, T. *Dangerous Diplomacy: The Story of Carl Lutz, Rescuer of 62,000 Hungarian Jews* (Grand Rapids, Mich.: William B. Eerdmans, 2000).

18. Swiebocki, *London Has Been Informed,* 12.

19. Kulka, "Five Escapes from Auschwitz," 206.

20. Neumann, *Im Schatten des Todes,* 166.

21. Conway, "First Report about Auschwitz," 133–151.

22. Mordowicz, B. "I Have Come Out Alive Twice from Auschwitz." *Yalkut Moreshet* (Oct 1968): 7–20 (Hebrew).

23. Braham, *Politics of Genocide.*

24. Mordowicz, "I Have Come Out Alive Twice from Auschwitz," 7–20.

TWO   THE INFORMED

1. Cesarani, D., ed. *Genocide and Rescue: The Holocaust in Hungary 1944.* (Oxford and New York: Berg, 1997).

2. Bauer, Y. "Gizi Fleischmann," in *Women in the Holocaust,* eds. D. Ofer and L. J. Weitzman (New Haven, Conn.: Yale University Press, 1998), 258.

3. Gutman and Rozett, *Encyclopedia of the Holocaust,* 1554.

4. Jelinek, Y. "Ustredna Zidov," in *Encyclopedia of the Holocaust,* eds. I. Gutman and R. Rozett (New York: Macmillan Publications, 1990), 1554–1555.

5. Bauer, *Jews for Sale?*

6. Bauer, "Gizi Fleischmann," 261.

7. Buchler, Y. "The Deportations of Slovakian Jews to the Lublin District of Poland in 1942." *Holocaust and Genocide Studies* 6, no. 2 (1991): 151–165.

8. Bauer, *Jews for Sale?*

9. Braham, *Politics of Genocide* (2000).

10. Gilbert, *Auschwitz and the Allies*, 209.

11. Bauer, *Jews for Sale?*

12. Braham, *Politics of Genocide;* Freudiger, F. "Five Months," in *The Tragedy of Hungarian Jewry: Essays, Documents, Depositions*, ed. R. L. Braham (New York: Columbia University Press, 1986), 237–294.

13. Bauer, *Jews for Sale?*, 156–157.

14. Aronson, S. "The 'Quadruple Trap' and the Holocaust in Hungary," in *Genocide and Rescue: The Holocaust in Hungary 1944*, ed. D. Cesarani (New York: Berg, 1997), 93–121.

15. Bauer, *Rethinking the Holocaust.*

16. Braham, *Politics of Genocide.*

17. According to Conway, two years earlier, the Papal Apostolic Delegate in Slovakia, Monsignor Angelo Burzio, had sounded the alarm bells in Rome when he had called for and received a strong message from the pope concerning the deportation of Slovakia's Jews, which he then delivered to the Slovakian President, Monsignor Tiso, who happened to be a Catholic priest. Given his sympathies for the unfortunate victims of Nazi and Slovakian policy, it was not surprising that Burzio reacted strongly to this latest news about Auschwitz, delivered by one of those Jewish victims whose deportation he had earlier been unable to prevent. He asked his assistant, Monsignor Martilotti, who was on temporary assignment from Switzerland, to study the Vrba-Wetzler report and, if possible, to arrange to meet with its authors and gain a firsthand impression of its accuracy. Through mediation by Krasniansky, such a meeting was arranged. Conway, "First Report about Auschwitz," 145. (Conway 1979, 1984, 1986.)

18. Baron, "Myth and Reality of Rescue," 171–208.

19. Gilbert, *Auschwitz and the Allies*, 262. See also Neumann, *Im Schatten des Todes.*

20. Karny, M. "The Vrba and Wetzler Report," in *Anatomy of the Auschwitz Death Camp*, eds. I. Gutman and M. Berenbaum (Bloomington: Indiana University Press, 1994), 553–568 (p. 566).

21. Gilbert, *Auschwitz and the Allies*, 234.

22. Swiebocki, *London Has Been Informed.*

23. Ibid.

24. Czech, D. *Kalenderium der Ereignisse in Konzentrations Lager 1935–1945* (Hamburg: Rowolt, 1989).

25. Gilbert, *Auschwitz and the Allies.*

26. Ibid., 233. See also Olivova, V. "Edvard Benes: Odsun Nemcu." Kniznice spolecnosti Edvard Benes. Prague. 8 (1995): 89–90.

27. Conway, "Holocaust in Hungary," 1–48; Levai, *Zsidosors europaban.*

28. Gilbert, *Auschwitz and the Allies.*

29. Bauer, " Conclusion: The Holocaust in Hungary," 193–209; Levai, *Zsidosors europaban.*

30. Dobbs, *Madeleine Albright: A Twentieth-Century Odyssey* (New York: Henry Holt and Co., 1999): 90–91.

31. Yahil, L. *The Holocaust: The Fate of European Jewry, 1932–1945* (New York: Oxford University Press, 1990).

32. Braham, *Politics of Genocide,* 276, note 53.

33. Conway, "First Report about Auschwitz," 133–151; Vrba, "Preparations for the Holocaust in Hungary" (1997), 227–279.

34. Braham, *Politics of Genocide* (2000).

35. Medford, R. "Letter to the Editor: New Evidence Concerning Ben-Gurion's Response to the Holocaust," *Journal of Genocide Research* 3, no. 3 (2001): 507–510.

36. Yad Vashem refused to honor Maria Szekely posthumously as a righteous Gentile. Her son in Budapest received a letter praising her from Yad Vashem.

37. "This [testimony about the translation] strengthens the theory," concludes Bauer, "that Kasztner had the information, but not the protocols, in early May and that the protocols reached Budapest some time in early June, too late to have any effect on the deportations, which started, let me repeat, on May 14." Bauer, *Rethinking the Holocaust.*

38. Bauer, *Jews for Sale?,* 157.

39. Braham, *Politics of Genocide* (2000); Milland, G. "The BBC Hungarian Service and the Final Solution in Hungary," *Historical Journal of Film, Radio and Television* 18, no. 3 (1998): 353–373.

40. Conway, "First Report about Auschwitz," 133–151. See also Conway, "Der Holocaust in Ungarn," 179–212; Bauer, *Rethinking the Holocaust,* 238.

41. Dreisziger, N. F. "Miklos Horthy and the Second World War: Some Historiographical Perspectives," *Hungarian Studies Review* 33, no. 1 (1996): 5–16 (p. 7).

42. Bauer, "Conclusion: The Holocaust in Hungary," 204, see also note 1.

43. Cesarani, *Genocide and Rescue.*

44. Weitz, Y. *The Man Who Was Murdered Twice* (Tel Aviv: Keter Publishing, 1995), 25.

45. Lang, J. V. and C. Sibyll. *Eichmann Interrogated: Transcripts from the Archives of the Israeli Police* (New York: Farrar Straus & Giroux, 1983), 201.

46. Ibid., 202.

47. Braham and Miller, *Nazis' Last Victims.*

48. Ibid.

49. Braham, *Politics of Genocide* (1981).

50. Pearlman, M. *The Capture and Trial of Adolf Eichmann* (London: Weidenfeld and Nicolson, 1963), 356–357.

51. Bauer, *Jews for Sale?,* 154.

52. Ibid.

53. Quoted in Robinson, J. *And the Crooked Shall Be Made Straight: The Eichmann Trial, the Jewish Catastrophe, and Hannah Arendt's Narrative* (Philadelphia: The Jewish Publication Society of America, 1965), 176–177.

54. Braham, *Politics of Genocide* (1981), 792.

55. Freudiger, "Five Months," 237–294 (p. 260).

56. Ibid., emphasis added.

57. Braham, *Politics of Genocide* (1981), 711.

58. Erez, T. "Hungary: Six Days in July 1944," *Holocaust and Genocide Studies* 3, no. 1 (1988): 37–53.

59. Freudiger, "Five Months," 257, emphasis added.

60. Ibid., 253.

61. Ibid., 272.

62. Ibid., 277, emphasis added.

63. Braham, *Politics of Genocide* (1981), 711.

64. Ibid., 792.

65. Pearlman, *Capture and Trial of Adolf Eichmann,* 357.

66. Ultra-Orthodox historians, for example, trying to cope with the morally problematic behavior of some of their informed leading rabbis, used various strategies: First, they erased shameful stories and accusations of surviving victims from their textbooks. Second, they dissociated their leaders' acts from the events, arguing that the leaders could not have done otherwise than flee, because they had been commanded to do so in a dream. Third, they ascribed to the ultra-Orthodox leaders some unique form of knowledge that dictated to them that they had to survive in order to establish new yeshivas.

Porat, D. "'Amalek collaborator': The Accusation of the Ultra Orthodox toward the Zionism in Israel during the 80th," in *Memory and Awareness of the Holocaust in Israel,* ed. Y. Rappel (Tel Aviv: The Ministry of Defense Publishing, 1998) (Hebrew).

67. Pearlman, *Capture and Trial of Adolf Eichmann,* 358.

THREE THE UNINFORMED

1. See Aronson, S. "Rezso Kasztner's Pandora Box," *Davar Hashavua,* September, 10, 1993 and Aronson, S. "Kasztner: The Trap. New Light on Joel Brand's Mission," *Davar Hashavua,* September, 24, 1993 (Hebrew). Also Bauer, *Jews for Sale?*

2. Braham, *Politics of Genocide,* 209.

3. Bauer, *Jews for Sale?;* Breitman, R. "Nazi Jewish Policy in 1944," in *Genocide and Rescue,* ed. D. Cesarani (New York: Berg, 1997), 77–92; Porat, D. *The Blue and the Yellow Stars of David: The Zionist Leadership in Palestine and the Holocaust, 1939–1945* (Cambridge, Mass.: Harvard University Press, 1990).

4. Pearlman, *Capture and Trial of Adolf Eichmann,* 360.

5. Ibid., 359.

6. Braham, *Politics of Genocide* (1981), 952.

7. Gilbert, *Auschwitz and the Allies,* 205.

8. Bauer, *Jews for Sale?*

9. Weitz, *Man Who Was Murdered Twice.*

10. Bauer, *Jews for Sale?;* Weitz, Y. "Between Warsaw and Budapest: On the Problem of Fighting in the Kasztner Trial." *Studies on the Holocaust* 5 (1995): 309–332; Weitz, *Man Who Was Murdered Twice.*

11. Braham, *Politics of Genocide* (1981), 955

12. See Biss, A. *A Million Jews to Save* (London: Hutchinson, 1973; South Brunswick, N.J.: A.S. Barnes, 1975) (Translated from German); Bauer, *Jews for Sale?;* Cesarani, *Genocide and Rescue;* Braham, *Politics of Genocide* (1981); Braham, *Politics of Genocide* (2000)—in this order.

13. Bauer, *Jews for Sale?,* 208.

14. Weitz, *Man Who Was Murdered Twice.*

15. Hecht, *Perfidy,* 78.

16. Muller-Tupath, K. *Reichsfuhrers gehorsamster Becher: Eine deutsche Karriere* (Fulda: Konkret Litteratur Verlag, 1982).

17. Cesarani, *Genocide and Rescue*, 15.
18. Bauer, *Jews for Sale?*
19. Weitz, *Man Who Was Murdered Twice*, 23 (author's translation from Hebrew).
20. Ibid., 192.
21. Hecht, *Perfidy*, 105–106.
22. Ibid., 107.
23. Robinson, *And the Crooked Shall Be Made Straight*, 180, emphasis added.
24. Gutman and Rozett, *Encyclopedia of the Holocaust*, 303, emphasis added.
25. Braham, *Politics of Genocide*, 972–973.
26. Bauer, "Anmerkungen zum 'Auschwitz-Bericht' von Rudolf Vrba," 297–307.
27. Braham, *Politics of Genocide*, 629.
28. Ibid., 629.
29. Bauer, "Conclusion: The Holocaust in Hungary," 196.
30. Braham, *Politics of Genocide*, 629.
31. Ibid., 92.
32. Biss, *Million Jews to Save*.
33. Bauer, *Jews for Sale?*
34. Fatran, G. "The 'Working Group,'" *Holocaust and Genocide Studies* 8, no. 2 (1994): 164–201 (p. 201, emphasis added).
35. Gutman and Rozett, *Encyclopedia of the Holocaust*.
36. Klein, G. *Sentenced to Live: A Survivor's Memoir* (New York: Holocaust Library, 1988), 494.
37. Klein, G. *Pieta: Mitleid Compassion Agape Caritas* (Cambridge, Mass.: MIT Press, 1989), 129.
38. Zertal, I. *Death and the Nation: History, Memory, Politics* (Tel Aviv: Devir, 2002), 119.
39. Ibid. See also Bilsky, L. "Judging Evil in the Trial of Kasztner," *Law and History Review* 19, no. 1 (2001), 1–29.
40. Bilsky, "Judging Evil," 5.
41. Aronson, "Rezso Kasztner's Pandora Box" and "Kasztner: The Trap."
42. Weitz, *Man Who Was Murdered Twice*.
43. Segev, T. *The Seventh Million: The Israelis and the Holocaust* (New York: Hill and Wang, 1993), 306.
44. Ibid. Also, as has been noted by Zertal, Israel was not cleansed from the

Dybbuk of the Holocaust and the Judenrate question was not, and probably never will be, solved. Zertal, *Death and the Nation*, 133.

45. Tamir, S. *Son of This Land* (Tel Aviv: Zmora Bitan, 2002), 1084.

46. See also Ishoni-Beri, S. "The Kasztner Affair: Testifying on Behalf of War Criminals—An Attempt to Provide a Different Explanation," *Yalkut Moreshet* 59 (1995): 85–107 (Hebrew).

47. Bauer, *Jews for Sale?*, 250, emphasis added.

48. Ibid.

49. Gutman and Rozett, *Encyclopedia of the Holocaust*, 799.

50. *Ha'aretz*, April 28, 2000.

PART TWO   BETWEEN AUSCHWITZ AND JERUSALEM

1. See Baron, "Myth and Reality of Rescue from the Holocaust," 171–208; Baron, F. and S. Szenes. *Von Ungarn nach Auschwitz: Die verschwiegene Warnung* (Munster: Westfalisches Dampfboot, 1994); Braham and Miller, *Nazis' Last Victims;* Marrus, M. R. *The Holocaust in History* (Hanover, N.H.: Published for Brandeis University Press by University Press of New England, 1987); Reit-linger, G. *The Final Solution: The Attempt to Exterminate the Jews of Europe, 1939–1945* (South Brunswick, N.J.: T. Yoseloff, 1961, 1968); Swiebocki, *London Has Been Informed;* Wyman, *Abandonment of the Jews*.

2. Sakmyster, T. L. *Hungary's Admiral on Horseback: Miklos Horthy, 1918–1944* (New York: Columbia University Press, 1994).

3. Neufeld, M. J. and M. Berenbaum. *The Bombing of Auschwitz: Should the Allies Have Attempted It?* (New York: St. Martin's Press, 2000).

4. Gutman et al., *Holocaust and Its Significance*.

5. Bankier, D. *The Germans and the Final Solution: Public Opinion under Nazism* (Oxford, UK: Blackwell, 1992).

6. Bedurftig, F. "Nahaufnahme aus dem Inneren Kreis der Holle," in *Als Kanada in Auschwitz lag*, ed. R. Vrba (Munchen: Piper, 1999), 319–327.

7. McCullagh, B. C. "Bias in Historical Description, Interpretations, and Explanation," *History and Theory* 39, no. 1 (2000): 39–66 (p. 40).

8. Dobbs, *Madeleine Albright*.

9. Blackman, A. *Seasons of Her Life: A Biography of Madeleine Korbel Al-bright* (New York: Scribner, 1998), 16.

10. Brown-Smith, N. "Family Secrets," *Journal of Family Issues* 19, no. 1

(1998): 20–42 (p. 22); Erickson, P. "The Role of Secrecy in Complex Organizations," *Cornell Journal of Social Relations* 114 (1979): 121–138.
11. Bauer, Y. "The Past Will Not Go Away," in *The Holocaust and History: The Known, the Unknown, the Disputed, and the Reexamined*, eds. M. Berenbaum and A. Peck (Washington: United States Holocaust Memorial Museum, 1998).

FOUR MISNAMING

1. Neumann, *Im Schatten des Todes*, 166, 178, 181.
2. Conway, "Holocaust in Hungary," 1–48 and "Significance of the Vrba-Wetzler Report on Auschwitz-Birkenau," 395–431.
3. Krasniansky, *A Declaration under Oath.*
4. Rothkirchen, L. *Hurban Yahadut Slovakyan* (Jerusalem: Yad Vashem, 1961).
5. Braham, R. L. "The Rescue of the Jews of Hungary in Historical Perspective," in *The Historiography of the Holocaust Period*, eds. I. Gutman and G. Greif (Jerusalem: Yad Vashem, Achva Press, 1988).
6. Rothkirchen, L. "The Role of the Czech and Slovak Jewish Leadership in the Field of Rescue Work," in *Rescue Attempts during the Holocaust.* Proceedings of the Second Yad Vashem International Historical Conference, Jerusalem. April 8–11, 1974. (Jerusalem: Yad Vashem, 1974), 423–434 (p. 427).
7. Bauer, Y. *The Holocaust in Historical Perspective* (Seattle: University of Washington Press, 1978).
8. Braham and Miller, *Nazis' Last Victims.*
9. Porat, D. "The Greek Jews—An Example for the Relation between Awareness to Rescuing during the Holocaust 1939–1945," *Dapim: Studies on the Shoa* 8 (1990): 123–134 (p. 130) (Translated from Hebrew).
10. Porat, *Blue and Yellow Stars of David*, 215.
11. Gilbert, *Auschwitz and the Allies.*
12. Kohn and Cohen, "Auschwitz protocols and the expulsion of the Hungarian Jews," 203–212 (p. 205) (Hebrew).
13. Cohen, "The Holocaust Hungarian Jews in Light of the Research of Randolph Braham," 360–382 (p. 372).
14. Gutman and Rozett, *Encyclopedia of the Holocaust*, 115.

15. Laqueur, W. and J. T. Baumel. *The Holocaust* Encyclopedia (New Haven, Conn.: Yale University Press, 2001).

16. Gilbert, *Auschwitz and the Allies*, 196, figure 22; Swiebocki, *London Has Been Informed*, 34.

FIVE   MISREPORTING

1. Butz, A. R. *The Hoax of the Twentieth Century* (Richmond: Historical Review Press, 1977).

2. Neumann, *Im Schatten des Todes*.

3. Butz, *Hoax of the Twentieth Century*, 99.

4. Ibid., 96.

5. Kulka, "Five Escapes from Auschwitz," 212–237.

6. Ibid.

7. See Conway, J. S. "Der Auschwitz-Bericht von April 1944," *Zeitgeschichte* 8: 413–442.

8. Faurisson, R. "How the British Obtained the Confessions of Rudolf Hoss," *Journal of Historical Review* 7, no. 4 (1986–1987): 389–401.

9. Bauer, *Jews for Sale?*

10. Neumann, *Im Schatten des Todes;* Porat, "The Greek Jews" and *Blue and Yellow Stars of David;* Rothkirchen, L. "The Final Solution in Its Last Stages," in *The Catastrophe of European Jewry*, eds. I. Gutman and L. Rothkirchen (Jerusalem: Yad Vashem, 1976).

11. Gutman, I. and M. Berenbaum. *Anatomy of the Auschwitz Death Camp* (Bloomington: Published in association with the United States Holocaust Memorial Museum Washington, D.C., by Indiana University Press, 1994), vii.

12. Berenbaum and Peck, *Holocaust and History*, 833.

13. Bauer, *Holocaust in Historical Perspective;* Bauer, *Jews for Sale?;* Bauer, *Rethinking the Holocaust;* Gutman, I. *Shoah Vezikaron* (Jerusalem: Yad Vashem and Merkaz Shazr publication, 1999); Rothkirchen, "Czech and Slovak Wartime Jewish Leadership," 629–646.

14. Lipstadt, *Beyond Belief,* 233. For Irving, see Internet: Historian's Holocaust Libel Suit Dismissed by Judge in London, April 11, 2000.

15. "There was a place called the ramp where the trains with the Jews were coming in. They were coming in day and night. . . . sometimes one per day and sometimes five per day, from all sorts of places in the world. I worked there from August 18, 1942 to June 7, 1943.

I saw those transports rolling one after another, and I have seen at least two hundred of them. . . . I have seen it so many times that it became a routine. Constantly, people from the heart of Europe were disappearing and they were arriving to the same place with the same ignorance of the fate of the previous transport.
I knew . . . that within a couple of hours after they arrived there, ninety percent would be gassed."
U.S. Holocaust Museum.
  16. Linn, *What Do Our Students Know about Holocaust Heroes?*

SIX   MISCREDITING

  1. Lanik, J. *Oswiecim, hrobka styroch millionov ludi* [Auschwitz, Tomb of Four Million People] (Kosice: Vydalo Poverenictve SNR, 1946).
  2. Lanik, J. *Co Dante nevidel* [What Dante Did Not See] (Bratislava: Obzor, 1964).
  3. Vrba and Bestic, *Escape from Auschwitz.*
  4. Yahil, *Holocaust,* 638.
  5. Bauer, *Jews for Sale?;* Fatran, "The 'Working Group,'" 164–201; Fatran, G. "Letters to the Editor: Response," *Holocaust and Genocide Studies* 9, no. 2 (1995): 272–276; Kulka, "Escape of Jewish Prisoners."
  6. Fatran, "The 'Working Group,'" 200.
  7. Feeney, T. J. "Expert Psychological Testimony on Credibility Issues," *Military Law Review* 115 (1987): 121–177.
  8. Fatran, G. *The Jewish Center UZ: An Organization of Collaborators or a Rescue Group, the Jews of Slovakia—1938–1944* (Jerusalem: Hebrew University Press, 1988), 127
  9. Fatran, G. *Struggle for Surviving? The Leadership of Slovakian Jews in the Holocaust 1938–1944* (Tel Aviv: Moreshet, 1992), 170 (Hebrew).
  10. Bauer, "Anmerkungen zum 'Auschwitz-Bericht' von Rudolf Vrba," 297–307; Gilbert, *Auschwitz and the Allies;* Karny, "Vrba and Wetzler Report," 553–568.
  11. LaCapra, D. *History and Criticism* (Ithaca, N.Y.: Cornell University Press, 1985), 141.
  12. Ibid.
  13. Bauer, Y. *The Holocaust: Some Historical Aspects* (Tel Aviv: Hapoalim, 1987), 175, 146 (Hebrew).

14. Bauer, "Anmerkungen zum 'Auschwitz-Bericht' von Rudolf Vrba," 297–307 (p. 297).

15. Vrba, "Die Missachtete Warnung," 1–25.

16. Bauer, "Anmerkungen zum 'Auschwitz-Bericht' von Rudolf Vrba," 303, note 18.

17. Karny, "Vrba and Wetzler Report," 553–568. In the 2003 Hebrew version of their book *Anatomy of the Auschwitz Death Camp*, Gutman and Berenbaum assume a similar position of clouding (see page 480, ndeg).

18. Pieters, J. "New Historicism: Postmodern Historiography between Narrativism and Heterology," *History and Theory* 39, no. 1 (2000): 21–38 (p. 36).

19. Fatran, "The 'Working Group,'" 164–201 and "Letters to the Editor," 272–276.

20. Conway, "Holocaust in Hungary," 1–48; Conway, "Significance of the Vrba-Wetzler Report on Auschwitz-Birkenau," 395–431; Gilbert, *Jewish Resistance: The Unknown Heroes*.

21. Kraus, O. and E. Kulka. *The Death Mills of Auschwitz* (Jerusalem: Jerusalem Post Printing, 1960); Kulka, "Five Escapes from Auschwitz," 212–237.

22. Kulka, "Escape of Jewish Prisoners."

23. Kulka, "Five Escapes from Auschwitz," 212–237 (p. 236). It must be noted that in his 1984 article Kulka reports that Vrba's criticism of their wartime leadership so angered the Slovak activists that they protested vehemently in three letters they sent to the Czechoslovak immigrants organization in Israel.

24. *Voices: Newsletter of the Czechoslovak Jewish Communities Sound Archive*, New York, May 1991, p. 1, p. 4, emphasis added. Davis concludes her letter: "[Your] book should be on the bookshelf of everyone of Czechoslovak Jewish family background. Most of my own close family were killed in Auschwitz in October 1944. I owe you an immeasurable debt for trying to save them."

25. See Bauer, *Jews for Sale?* and Gutman and Berenbaum, *Anatomy of the Auschwitz Death Camp*.

26. Crismore, A. "The Rhetoric of Textbooks: Metadiscourse," *Journal of Curriculum Studies* 16, no. 3 (1984): 279–296; Wineburg, S. S. "On the Reading of Historical Texts: Notes on the Breach between School and Academy," *American Educational Research Journal* 28 (1991): 495–519.

27. Ibid., 511.
28. Ibid., 498.
29. Young, J. E. *The Texture of Memory: Holocaust Memorials and Meaning* (New Haven: Yale University Press, 1993), 5.

SEVEN   MISREPRESENTING

1. Bauer, *Jews for Sale?*, 72.
2. Czech, *Kalenderium*.
3. Ibid., 297.
4. Bauer, *Jews for Sale?*; Braham, *Politics of Genocide* (2000).
5. Braham, *Politics of Genocide* (1981).
6. Bauer, "Anmerkungen zum 'Auschwitz-Bericht' von Rudolf Vrba," 297–307.
7. Shonfeld, M. *The Holocaust Victims Accuse: Documents and Testimony on Jewish War Criminals* (Brooklyn, N.Y.: Bnei Yeshivos, 1977).
8. Vrba, "Preparations for the Holocaust in Hungary" (1998), 227–279; Vrba, "Preparations for the Holocaust in Hungary" (1997), 55–101.
9. Bauer, *Rethinking the Holocaust*, 229.
10. Bloxham, D. *Genocide on Trial: The War Crimes Trials and the Formation of Holocaust History and Memory* (New York: Oxford University Press, 2001).
11. Diner, D. "Cumulative Contingency: Historicizing Legitimacy on Israeli Discourse," *History and Memory* 7, no. 1 (1995): 147–170 (p. 157, emphasis in the original).
12. Ben Ami, *Hashtika*.
13. Gutman, *Shoah Vezikaron*.
14. Browning, C. *Nazi Policy, Jewish Workers, German Killers* (New York: Cambridge University Press, 2000), 115.

PART THREE   BETWEEN HISTORY AND MEMORY

1. Gross, J. T. *Neighbors: The Destruction of the Jewish Community in Jedwabne, Poland* (Princeton, N.J.: Princeton University Press, 2001), 168–169.

2. Schlant, E. *The Language of Silence: West German Literature and the Holocaust* (New York: Routledge, 1999).

EIGHT COOPERATING LEADERS

1. Soros, T. *Masquerade: Dancing around Death in Nazi-occupied Hungary* (Edinburgh: Canogate Books, 1965/2000), 17–18. See Hilberg, *Destruction of the European Jews.*

2. See Langer, L. L. *Holocaust Testimonies: The Ruins of Memory* (New Haven: Yale University Press, 1990); Langer, L. L. *Preempting the Holocaust* (New Haven: Yale University Press, 1998). See Robinson, *And the Crooked Shall Be Made Straight.*

3. Felman, S. "Theatres of Justice: Arendt in Jerusalem, the Eichmann Trial, and the Redefinition of Legal Meaning in the Wake of the Holocaust," *Theoretical Inquiries in Law* 1, no. 2 (2000): 465–507.

4. Feldman, H. R., ed. "'Eichmann in Jerusalem': An Exchange of Letters between Gershon Scholem and Hannah Arendt," in Hannah Arendt's *The Jew as Pariah: Jewish Identity and Politics in the Modern Age* (New York: Grove Press, 1978), 240–251 (p. 248).

5. Gutman and Rozett, *Encyclopedia of the Holocaust,* 762.

6. Bauer, *Jews for Sale?*

7. Diner, D. "Historical Understanding and Counterrationality: The Judenrat as Epistemological Vantage," in *Probing the Limits of Representation: Nazism and the "Final Solution,"* ed. S. Friedlander (Cambridge, Mass.: Harvard University Press, 1992), 128–142 (p. 139).

8. See Kirmayer, L. J. "Landscape of Memory: Trauma, Narrative and Dissociation," in *Tense Past: Cultural Essays in Trauma and Memory,* eds. P. Antze and M. Lambek (New York: Routledge, 1996).

9. Gutman and Rozett, *Encyclopedia of the Holocaust,* 1555, emphasis added.

10. Neumann, *Im Schatten des Todes.*

11. Diner, "Historical Understanding and Counterrationality," 141.

12. The phrase is taken from Brunner, J. "Pride and Memory: Nationalism, Narcissism and the Historians' Debates in Germany and Israel," in *History and Memory: Studies in Representation of the Past. Passing into History: Nazism and the Holocaust Beyond Memory,* ed. G. Arad-Neeman. In the Honor of Saul Friedlander on his 65th birthday: (1997), 256–300 (p. 284).

13. Lowenthal, D. *The Past Is a Foreign Country* (Cambridge, Mass.: Cambridge University Press, 1985), 214, 218.

14. Bauer, *Jews for Sale?*, 73, emphasis added.

15. Robinson, *And the Crooked Shall Be Made Straight*, 175, emphasis added.

16. Ibid., 79, emphasis added.

17. Ibid., 61, emphasis added.

18. Rothkirchen, "Czech and Slovak Wartime Jewish Leadership," 629–646 (p. 644).

19. Spitzer, *I Did Not Want to Be a Jew*, 119.

20. See Hyden, W. "The Historical Text as Literary Artifact," in *The Writing of History: literary from the Historical Understanding*, eds. R. H. Canary and H. Kozicki (Madison: University of Wisconsin Press, 1978).

21. Rothkirchen (1998), 637, 633, 629, accordingly.

22. Kohn and Cohen, "Auschwitz Protocols and the Expulsion of the Hungarian Jews," 203–212 (p. 205, emphasis added) (Hebrew).

23. Cohen, "Holocaust Hungarian Jews in Light of the Research of Randolph Braham," 381, emphasis added.

24. Cohen, A. "Resistance and Rescue in Hungary," in *Genocide and Rescue: The Holocaust in Hungary 1944*, ed. D. Cesarani (New York: Berg, 1997), 123–134 (p. 131, emphasis added).

25. Porat, D. "19 March to 19 July—What Did the Yishuv know?," in *Genocide and Rescue: The Holocaust in Hungary 1944*, ed. D. Cesarani (New York: Berg, 1997), 189.

26. Kertesz, I. *Sorstalansag* (Tel Aviv: Am Oved Publishing, 2002), 44 (Translation from Hebrew).

NINE RESISTING INDIVIDUALS

1. Quoted in Arad-Neeman, G. "Nazi Germany and the Jews: Reflection on a Beginning, a Middle and an Open End," *History and Theory* 9, no. 12 (1997): 409–433 (p. 411).

2. Lanik, *Co Dante nevidel*.

3. Langbein, *Menschen in Auschwitz*.

4. Lanik, *Co Dante nevidel*, 215.

5. Vrba and Bestic, *Escape from Auschwitz*, 221.

6. Langbein, *Against All Hope;* Swiebocki, *London Has Been Informed.* See also Krasaniansky, *A Declaration under Oath,* 20.

7. See Garlinski, J. *Fighting Auschwitz: The Resistance Movement in the Concentration Camp* (London: Julian Friedmann Publishers, 1975).

8. Vrba and Bestic, *Escape from Auschwitz,* 154

9. Cohen, "The Holocaust Hungarian Jews," 360–382.

10. Langbein, *Menschen in Auschwitz.*

11. Bauer, Y. *They Chose Life: Jewish Resistance in the Holocaust* (New York: American Jewish Committee Institute of Human Relations, 1973), 33, emphasis in the original.

12. Rothkirchen, L. "Escape Routes and Contacts during the War," in *Jewish Resistance during the Holocaust.* Proceedings of the Conference on Manifestations of Jewish Resistance, Jerusalem, April 7–11, 1968, ed. M. Kohn (Jerusalem: Yad Vashem, 1971), 409–414 (p. 410).

13. *Voices: Newsletter of the Czechoslovak Jewish Communities Sound Archive,* New York, May 1991, p. 5.

14. Brugioni, D. A. "The Aerial Photos of the Auschwitz-Birkenau Extermination Complex," in *The Bombing of Auschwitz: Should the Allies Have Attempted It?,* eds. M. J. Neufeld and M. Berenbaum (New York: St. Martin's Press, 2000), 56.

15. Diner, "Cumulative Contingency," 149.

16. Ibid., 164.

17. Bhabha, H. K. *Nation and Narration* (London: Routledge, 1999), 292.

18. Anderson, B. R. *Imagined Communities: Reflections on the Origin and Spread of Nationalism* (London: Verso, 1995).

19. Zertal, I. *Death and the Nation,* 56–57 (Translation from Hebrew).

20. Linn, *What Do Our Students Know About Holocaust Heroes?*

TEN   MEDIATING HISTORIANS

1. Langbein, *Against All Hope,* 256–257.

2. Bauer, "Conclusion: The Holocaust in Hungary," 193–209.

3. Fatran, *Struggle for Surviving?,* 235.

4. Ibid., 237, translation from Hebrew.

5. Bauer, *Rethinking the Holocaust,* Fatran, "The 'Working Group,'" 164–201.

6. Fatran, "The 'Working Group,'" 164–201; Fatran, "Letters to the Editor," 272–276.

7. In addition, twenty-nine other Jews from Palestine were sent by the Yishuv leaders to help the Diaspora Jews and parachuted into occupied Europe in March 1944 under British sponsorship.

8. Braham, *Politics of Genocide,* 933.

9. Ibid. See also Klein, *Pieta;* Soros, *Masquerade.*

10. Bauer, *Jews for Sale?*

11. Gutman and Rozett, *Encyclopedia of the Holocaust;* Laor, D. "Theatrical Interpretation of the Shoah: Image and Counter-image," in *Staging the Holocaust: The Shoah in Drama and Performance,* ed. C. Schumacher (New York: Cambridge University Press, 1998), 94–110.

12. Baumel, "The 'Parachutist's Mission' from a Gender Perspective," 105.

13. Braham, *Politics of Genocide,* 219.

14. Laor, "Theatrical Interpretation of the Shoah," 94–110.

15. Gutman and Rozett, *Encyclopedia of the Holocaust.*

16. Vrba and Bestic, *Escape from Auschwitz,* 252.

17. Bauer, "Anmerkungen zum 'Auschwitz-Bericht' von Rudolf Vrba," 297–307; Cohen, A. "Historia shel kishlonot," *Dapim: Studies on the Shoa* 9 (1991): 33–72 (Hebrew).

18. Chatz, T., I. Staub, and H. Lavine. "On the Varieties of National Attachment: Blind versus Constructive Patriotism," *Political Psychology* 20, no. 1 (1999): 151–174.

19. Dawidowicz, L. *Holocaust and the Historians* (Cambridge, Mass.: Harvard University Press, 1981), 134, note 4.

20. Diner, "Cumulative Contingency," 147–170 (p. 152).

21. Brigham, "Monument or Memorial? The Wall and the Politics of Memory," *Historical Reflections* 25, no. 1 (1999): 165–175 (p. 166); Kramer, J. *The Politics of Memory* (New York: Random House, 1996).

22. Brigham, R. K. "Monument or Memorial?, 165–175 (p. 166); Kramer, *Politics of Memory.*

23. Bartov, *Murder in Our Midst,* 88.

24. Bauer, *Rethinking the Holocaust,* 55.

25. Friedlander, S. "Dimensions of the Holocaust: Remarks on Two Studies," *Yad Vashem Studies* 22 (1992): 1–16 (p. 1).

26. Michman, D. *Ha-Sho'ah ve-hikrah: hamsagah, minuah ve-sugyot yesod*

(Tel Aviv: Moreshet Publication, 1998), 21 (Hebrew). Exclamation mark in the original, 107–108, author's translation.

27. For Arendt, see Gutman and Rozett, *Encyclopedia of the Holocaust.* For Melkman, see Stauber, R. *Lesson for This Generation* (Jerusalem: Yad Ben-Zvi Press, 2000), 219.

ELEVEN   CORRUPT SAVIORS

1. Becker, J. *Jacob the Liar* (New York: Harcourt Brace Jovanovich, 1975).
2. Tushnet, *Pavement of Hell.*
3. Bauer, *They Chose Life,* 43, emphasis added.
4. Trunk, *Judenrat;* Tushnet, *Pavement of Hell.*
5. Ibid., 46.
6. Ibid., 48, emphasis added.
7. Ibid., 61.
8. Eichengreen, L. *Rumkowski and the Orphans of Lodz.* (San Francisco: Mercury House, 2000).
9. Bauer, *They Chose Life,* 43–44, emphasis added.

TWELVE   POWERFUL KNOWERS

1. Gutman and Rozett, *Encyclopedia of the Holocaust,* 115.
2. Vrba and Bestic, *Escape from Auschwitz,* 150.
3. Bauer, *Holocaust in Historical Perspective.*
4. Bauer, *Jews for Sale?,* 72.
5. Bauer, "Conclusion: The Holocaust in Hungary," 197.
6. Fatran, *Struggle for Surviving?,* 237 (Translation from Hebrew).
7. Cohen, "The Holocaust Hungarian Jews," 360–382 (p. 381).
8. Soros, *Masquerade,* 65. Phone interview, March 3, 2001.
9. Cohen, "The Holocaust Hungarian Jews," 360–382.
10. Pink, I. "In the Path of Memory" (1996): 6.
11. Quoted in Kraus and Kulka, *Death Mills of Auschwitz,* 136, author's translation.
12. See the works of Foucault, M., particularly *Language, Counter-Memory, Practice: Selected Essays and Interviews* (Ithaca, N.Y.: Cornell University Press, 1977) and *The History of Sexuality,* vol 2: *The Use of Pleasure* (New York: Penguin Books, 1985).
13. Braham, "Rescue of the Jews of Hungary," 456.

14. Klein, *Sentenced to Live*, 72.
15. Ibid., 73.
16. Ibid., 77.
17. See Bauer, *Jews for Sale?;* Bauer, "Anmerkungen zum 'Auschwitz-Bericht' von Rudolf Vrba," 297–307; and Cesarani, *Genocide and Rescue.*
18. Isaacson, *Seed of Sarah*, 55.
19. Vrba and Bestic, *Escape from Auschwitz*, 186–188.
20. Langbein, *Menschen in Auschwitz*, 140–142.
21. Fiderkiewicz, *Brzezinka, Birkenau*, 246.
22. Vrba, R. and A. Bestic, *44070: The Conspiracy of the Twentieth Century* (Bellingham, Wash.: Star & Cross Publishing House, 1989).
23. Kulka, *Escape from Auschwitz*, 21.

PART FOUR   BETWEEN BANALITY AND POLITICS

1. Czech, *Kalendarium.*
2. Bauer, *Rethinking the Holocaust.*
3. Braham and Miller, *Nazis' Last Victims*, 17.
4. Ibid.
5. Cesarani, *Genocide and Rescue.*
6. Braham and Miller, *Nazis' Last Victims*, 91.
7. Gray, L. and L. Alcoff. "Survivor Discourse: Transgression of Recuperation?" *Signs: Journal of Women in Culture and Society* 18, no. 2 (1993): 260–290.

THIRTEEN   "REAL" HISTORIANS AND "TRUE" STORIES

1. Bauer, Y., H. Yablonka, Y. Jelinek, N. Akiva, G. Fatran, E. Frider, J. Conway, L. Rothkirchen, J. Spitzer, eds. *Leadership in Time of Distress: The Working Group in Slovakia, 1942–1944* (Kibbutz Dalia: Maarechet, 2001), 11–12. Introduction by Giora Amir. Translation from Hebrew.
2. Bauer, *Rethinking the Holocaust*, 15.
3. Ibid., 213.
4. Zur, Y. "Carnival Fears: Moroccan Immigrants and the Ethnic Problem in the Young State of Israel," *Journal of Israeli History* 18, no. 1 (1997): 73–103 (p. 76).
5. Shaked, M. "Historia bebeit hamishpat vebeit hamishpat bahistoris:

piskei din bemishpat Kasztner vehanarativim shel hazikaron [History in the court and the court in history: verdicts in Kasztner's trial and the narratives of memory], *Alpayim* 20 (2000): 36–80 (p. 71) (Hebrew).

6. On the Philosophy of History, published in the English version of his *Illuminations*, quoted in Hutton's "Recent Scholarship on Memory and History," *The History Teacher* 33, no. 4: 534–548 (p. 544).

7. See *Jews for Sale?*, page 200 for number of passengers.

8. See note 12 in Bauer's 1997 article "Anmerkugen zum."

9. Braham and Miller, *Nazis' Last Victims*, 91.

10. Bauer, *Rethinking the Holocaust*, 238.

11. See Bauer, "Anmerkungen zum 'Auschwitz-Bericht' von Rudolf Vrba," note 18. Gutman follows this pattern of clouding in the 2003 Hebrew version of his book *Anatomy of the Auschwitz Death Camp*, 480, note 9.

12. Bauer, *Rethinking the Holocaust*, 230, 230, 235, 237.

13. Ibid., 82.

14. Cesarani, *Genocide and Rescue*, 15.

15. Friedlander, S. "Trauma, Memory and Transference," in *Holocaust Remembrance*, ed. G. H. Hartman (Oxford: Blackwell, 1994), 252–263 (p. 262).

16. LaCapra, *History and Criticism*, 72–73.

17. Bauer, *Rethinking the Holocaust*, 102.

18. See Doerr, K. *Holocaust Survivors and the German Language: Women Remember.* Paper delivered at the 29th Annual Scholars Conference on the Holocaust and the Churches, "The Burdens of History: Post-Holocaust Generations in Dialogue," Nassau Community College, Garden City, N.Y., March 6–9, 1999; and Michael, R. and K. Doerr. *Nazi-Deutsch / Nazi-German: An English Lexicon of the Language of the Third Reich* (Westport, Conn.: Greenwood Press, 2002).

19. Bauer, *Rethinking the Holocaust*, 104.

20. Ibid.

21. Bauer, Y. "Daniel J. Goldhagen's View of the Holocaust," in *Hyping the Holocaust. Scholars Answer Goldhagen*, ed. Franklin H. Littell (Cumming & Hathaway Publishers, 1997), 59–72.

22. Bauer, *Rethinking the Holocaust*, 111, emphasis added.

23. Personal communication, June 10, 2000.

24. Bauer, *Rethinking the Holocaust*, 110.

25. Ibid.

26. Bauer, "Anmerkungen zum 'Auschwitz-Bericht' von Rudolf Vrba," 297.
27. Ibid., 111.

FOURTEEN NAKED VICTIMS, DRESSED-UP MEMORIES

1. Boyarin, J., ed. *Remapping Memory: The Politics of Time Space* (Minneapolis: University of Minnesota Press, 1994); Geyer, M. "The Politics of Memory in Contemporary Germany," in *Radical Evil*, ed. J. Copjec (London: Verso, 1996); Herf, J. *Divided Memory: The Nazi Past in the Two Germanys* (Cambridge, Mass.: Harvard University Press, 1997); Kramer, *Politics of Memory*.

2. LaCapra, D. *History and Memory after Auschwitz* (Ithaca, N.Y.: Cornell University Press, 1998), I.

3. Sakmyster, *Hungary's Admiral on Horseback*.

4. Fatran, *The Jewish Center UZ*.

5. Wolin, R. "The Ambivalences of German-Jewish Identity: Hannah Arendt in Jerusalem," *History and Memory* 8, no. 2 (1996): 9–34; Zertal, I. "Hannah Arendt in Jerusalem," *Fifty to Forty-eight: Critical Moments in the History of the State of Israel—Special Issue of Theory and Criticism* 12/13 (1999): 159–167.

6. Ash, T. G. "The Truth about Dictatorship," *The New York Review of Books*. February 19, 1998, 35–40.

7. Fatran, "The 'Working Group,'" 192, emphasis added.

8. Klein, *Pieta*, 130, 131.

9. Langbein, *Against All Hope*, 497.

10. Hutton, P. H. *History as an Art of Memory* (University of Vermont, published by Hanover, N.H.: University Press of New England, 1993).

11. Levy, D. "The Future of the Past: Historiographical Disputes and Competing Memories in Germany and Israel," *History and Theory* 38, no. 1 (1999): 51–66; Schlant, *The Language of Silence*.

12. Lentin, R. "Renewed Conquering of the Territories of Silence," in *Memory and Awareness of the Holocaust in Israel*, ed. Y. Rappel (Tel Aviv: The Ministry of Defense Publishing, 1998) (Hebrew); Smith, B. G. *The Gender of History: Men, Women, and Historical Practice* (Cambridge, Mass.: Harvard University Press, 1998); Zerubavel, Y. *Recovered Roots: Collective Memory and*

the Making of Israeli National Tradition (Chicago: University of Chicago Press, 1995).

13. Pieters, "New Historicism," 35.

14. Hilberg, R. *The Politics of Memory: The Journey of a Holocaust Historian* (Chicago: Ivan R. Dee, 1996), 66.

15. Friedlander, *Nazi Germany and the Jews.*

16. Arendt, *Eichmann in Jerusalem;* Cole, *Selling the Holocaust;* Gorny, Y. *Between Auschwitz and Jerusalem* (London and Portland, Ore.: Vallentine Mitchell, 2003) (Translated from Hebrew); Novick, *Holocaust in American Life.*

17. Bauer, "Gizi Fleischmann," 262, emphasis added.

INDEX

Albright, Madeleine, 31, 138n9
Arendt, Hannah, 6, 9–11, 13, 74, 76, 79,
  92, 119, 127n1, 130n1, 135n53, 144n4,
  148n27, 151n5
Auschwitz protocols, 32–33, 38, 60, 81,
  92, 100, 113, 134n37, 139n12, 145n22.
  See also Vrba-Wetzler report
Auschwitz report. *See* Vrba-Wetzler report

Bauer, Yehuda, 27, 32–34, 36, 46, 58, 66–
  68, 70–71, 95, 97, 99–101, 107, 109–117,
  120–122, 128n1, 128n3, 129n6, 129n15,
  132n2, 134n37, 137n26, 139n11, 141
  n13, 142n16, 146n11, 149n1, 150n21
Becher, Kurt, 41–43, 49, 51–52, 136n16
Ben Ami, Yehoshua, 6, 71, 110, 130n19,
  143n12
Bergen-Belsen train. *See* Kasztner, train
Biss, Andreas, 42, 79–80, 136n12
Blood for trucks, 41
Brand, Hanzi, 34, 42, 71
Brand, Joel, 26, 34, 40–42, 79, 136n1

Cluj, 26–27, 41–42, 44–46, 50–51
Conway, John, 62, 67, 128n1, 132n21, 133
  n17, 134n27, 134n33, 134n40, 139n2,
  140n7, 142n20, 149n1

Deportation, 10, 17, 23, 35–38, 41, 45–
  46, 48, 53, 57, 68, 75, 78–79, 81, 86,
  88–89, 95–97, 102, 104, 109, 112–114,
  119, 123, 131n5, 133n7, 133n17, 134
  n37; train, 20, 36; list, 80

Eichmann, Adolf, 12–13, 20, 24, 27–28,
  34–36, 40–41, 43–44, 48–50, 76, 79–
  80; in Jerusalem: book, 7, 92, 130n20,

131n8, 131n10, 144n4, 152n16; trial,
  9,13, 38, 52, 58, 62, 76, 79, 85, 88, 92,
  131n12, 135n45, 135n50, 135n53, 135
  n65, 136n67, 136n4, 144n3

Family camp, 3, 15–16, 29, 31, 54
Fatran, Gila, 119, 137n34, 141n5, 141n8,
  141n9, 149n1
Fleischmann, Gizi, 25, 80, 123, 132n2
Freedom train. *See* Kasztner, train
Freudiger, Rabbi Filip von, 25–27, 36–
  39, 42, 71, 79, 133n12, 135n55

Gilbert, Martin, 59, 67, 128n1, 142n20
Goldhagen, Daniel, 115–117, 130n3, 150
  n21
Good Shepherd Mission, 32
Greenwald, Malkiel, 49
Gross, Jan T., 73–74, 143n1
Gutman, Israel, 68, 72, 115, 128n1, 129n5,
  129n14 133n20, 139n5, 140n10, 140n13

Halevi, Benjamin, 13, 49–50
Hausner, Gideon, 13, 79
Hilberg, Raul, 9, 76; book (1961), 91–93,
  128n1, 131n5, 152n14
Horthy, Admiral Miklos, 28, 33–34, 38,
  53, 79, 97, 118, 134n41, 138n1
Hungarian Independent Movement, 32

Jewish Council, 113, 123, 131n6; Hungarian, 108; Slovak, 21, 23, 79, 82, 94, 100.
  See also Working Group
Judenrate (s., Judenrat), 9–12, 24, 27, 33,
  39, 45, 48–49, 76–78, 80–81, 91–92,
  102, 119, 131n6, 138n44, 144n7, 148n4
Juttner, Hans, 51–52

153

By Rudolf Vrba

I Cannot Forgive (with Alan Bestic)

First published in London, 1964, by Sidgwick and Jackson; first published in the United States, 1964, by Grove Press; first published in the German Federal Republic, 1964, by Rutten & Loening; first published in France, 1988, by Editions Ramsay. New expanded edition, *44070— The Conspiracy of the Twentieth Century,* first published in the United States, 1989, by Star & Cross. First published as *I Escaped from Auschwitz* in Israel, 1998, by Haifa University Press; in the United States, 2002, by Barricade Books

www.ingramcontent.com/pod-product-compliance
Lightning Source LLC
Chambersburg PA
CBHW020452100426
42813CB00031B/3336/J